AF488394

Life & Love

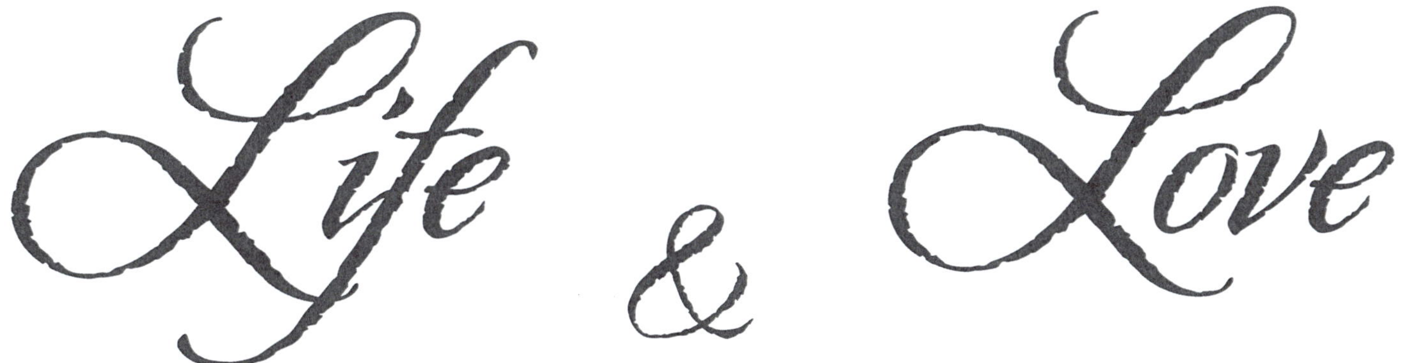

The Journey of Life and Love in Words and Images

MICHAEL CHASE

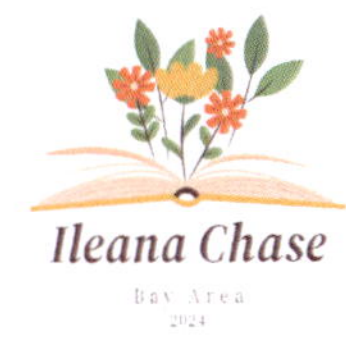

Ileana Chase

Bay Area
2024

Life & Love:

The Journey of Life and Love in Words and Images

ISBN: 979-8-9997136-0-5

Library of Congress Case Number: 1-14970342221

Photography © by Ileana Chase

First Edition: July 2025

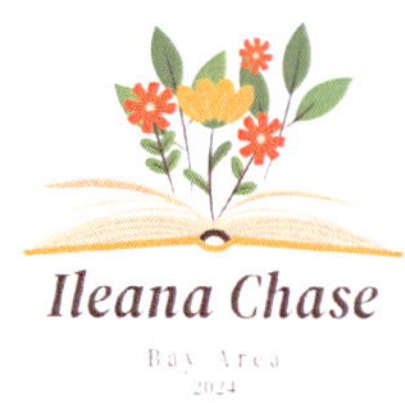

This book is dedicated to Ileana.

Your belief in me, your encouragement,

and your support made this book possible.

Foreword

How many times have you ever read a poem and wished you knew what the author was thinking when he wrote it, or the circumstances that inspired it? In this collection I not only give you a glimpse into my soul but also a glimpse into my mind as I share with you my experiences with Life and Love

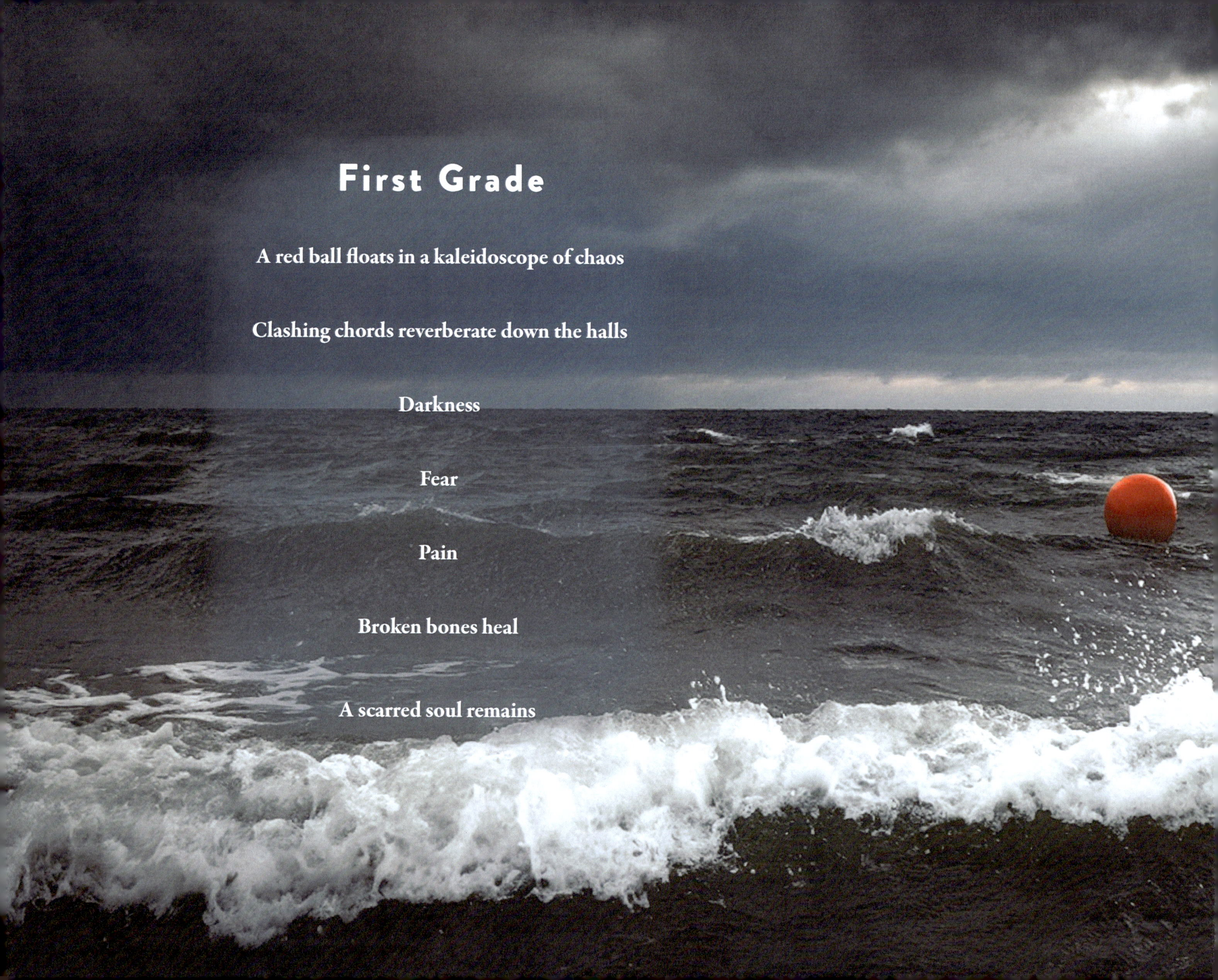

First Grade

A red ball floats in a kaleidoscope of chaos

Clashing chords reverberate down the halls

Darkness

Fear

Pain

Broken bones heal

A scarred soul remains

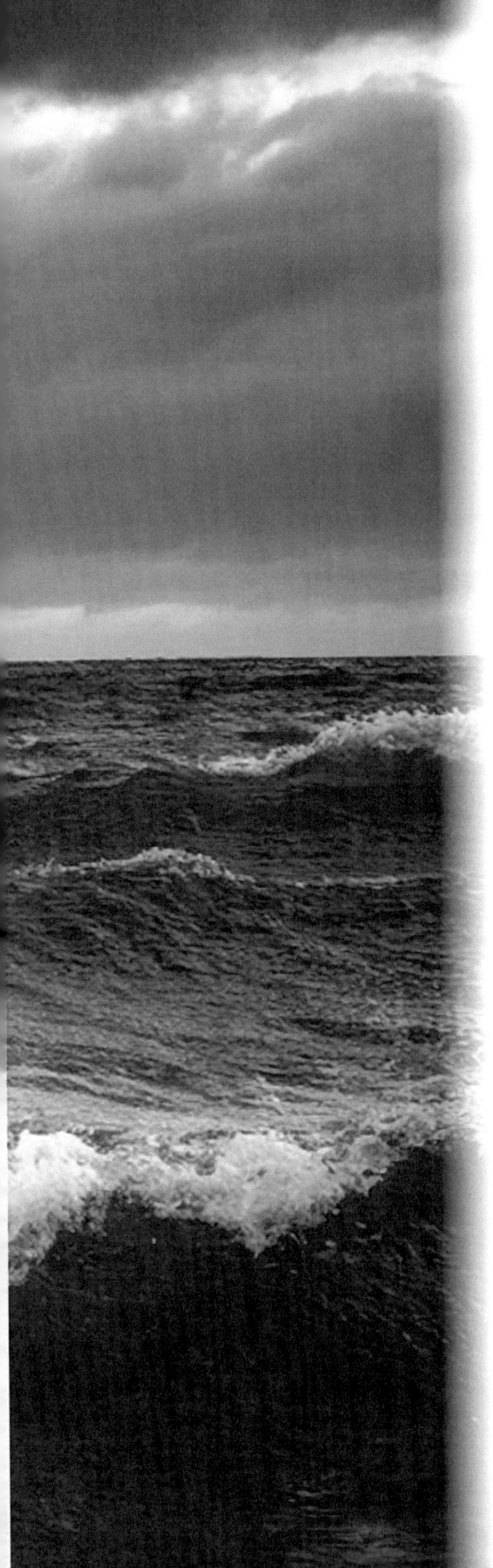

I magine a gray gloomy day in a small town in Iowa. A light drizzle has started to fall soaking everything in a mournful melancholy. Children in their classrooms going through their lessons as if by rote as the drizzle soaks through the window pane and into their hearts. Finally the bell sounds for recess but as the outside was blocked by the permeating gloom they were forced to spend it inside the gymnasium. An older part of the building that served as both basketball court and theater for the in-school productions of Wizard of Oz and the like. In the corner sat the old upright piano. A bit neglected and well-worn by the hundreds of students that passed through banging the keys whenever teachers weren't looking. Today the teachers were taking a break in the lunch room so the piano was unguarded. All the children from Kindergarten through Third Grade were packed into the gymnasium. Squeals of laughter, the squeak of tennis shoes on the hardwood, and the pounding of the keys on the old piano ricocheted and reverberated throughout the room. Then above it all came the clashing chord of all the keys on the piano being struck at the same time. In an attempt to gain better access to the keys that were up against the wall, children had wedged themselves between the wall and the piano forcing the piano to teeter on its missing caster and tumble over. The sound echoed down the hallway to the lunchroom and the teachers suddenly realized something terrible just happened. When they arrived they found me trapped beneath the piano.

After weeks in the hospital and some time in a wheelchair I recovered and life goes on, but it is always with me.

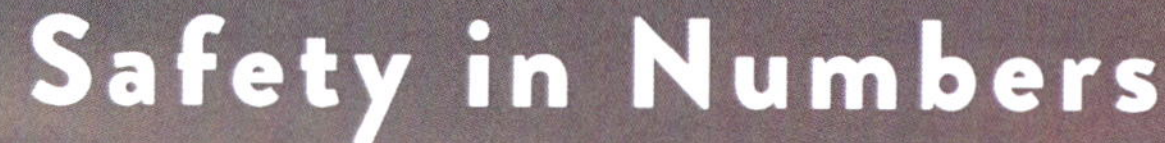

There is safety in numbers, this is true,
For one and one will always be two.
It has always been and will be forever more.
The same as two and two will always be four.

There is no room for interpretation or point of view,
Numbers do not feel more three than two.
One can't say that because two hurt one
they'll never again be combined.

It's absurd!
It's not done.

The rules of numbers are clearly defined,
there is no change with the passing of time.
There is safety in numbers,

yes, this is true.
They're the one constant in our universe,
not like me or you.

If two became one,
or I became you,
our universe would be lost.
Our lives would be through.

If one combines with two,
or I with you,
then we become three,
not one and two.
We lose our identity
and become something new.
Something wildly fun and exciting, that's true,
but when we separate,
am I me,
or am I you?

There is safety in numbers, we have seen this is true,
as long as one remains one,
and two remains two.
I remain me,
and you remain you.

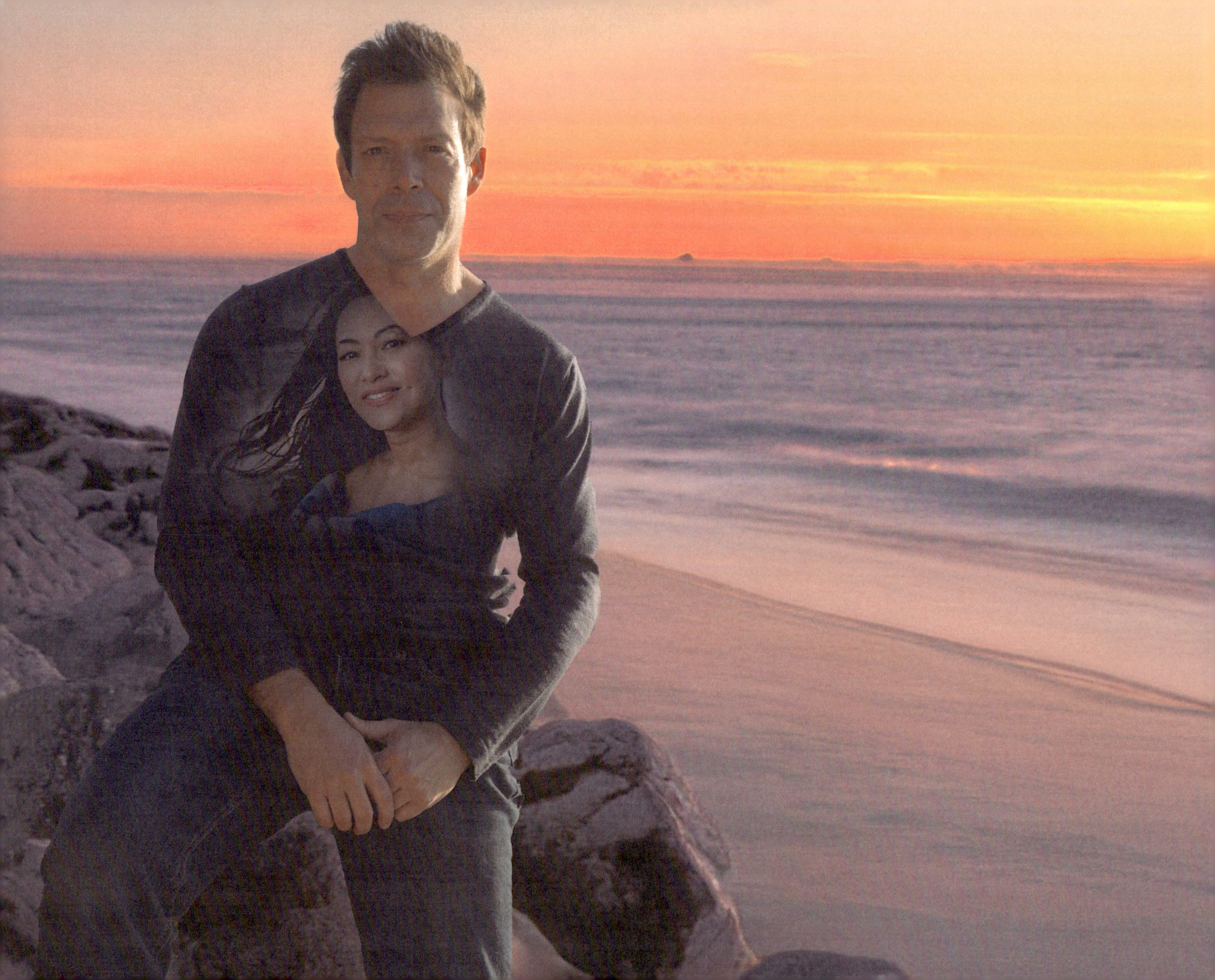

Mathematics has always held a certain sense of security for me. Numbers do not imply emotion. One cannot read the sentence, "One plus one equals two," and reach a different meaning just by emphasizing one word over another. Numbers do not offend, they just are. Words and literature, on the other hand, can excite strong emotion, indignation, disgust, they can hurt, they can elicit lusty thoughts and painful sorrow.

Choose the wrong word and friendships, even love, can be forever lost. Choose the wrong words and you can commit yourself to a path you dread. Then how do you get out of it? More words, more tangled webs of meaning. If I use the word "you" then it implies blame, "I" implies conceit, "they" implies lack of responsibility, "always" implies an inability to change and no recognition of the time when it wasn't so.

Words are dangerous. Words start wars. Words can push a person to suicide. But numbers are safe. You can know exactly what is meant by looking at a number, no guessing, no hesitation, no feeling. But not so with words.

Poetry is filled with words painting visions of two souls becoming one. A blissful coexistence greater than the sum of the parts. And a tragic end if one part should leave or be taken away. Relationships and emotions are as confusing and ambiguous as the meanings of words used between lovers.

"Togetherness," is one such word with hidden meanings. Can I still be myself if I'm together with you? What does it mean to be together as a couple? If we're not next to each other are we still together, do I have to somehow change now to reflect the "you" part of me that isn't standing here with me. Do all my "I's" turn to "we's", do my "me's" turn to "us"? Where did I go? Who is this staring back at me? Who are you?

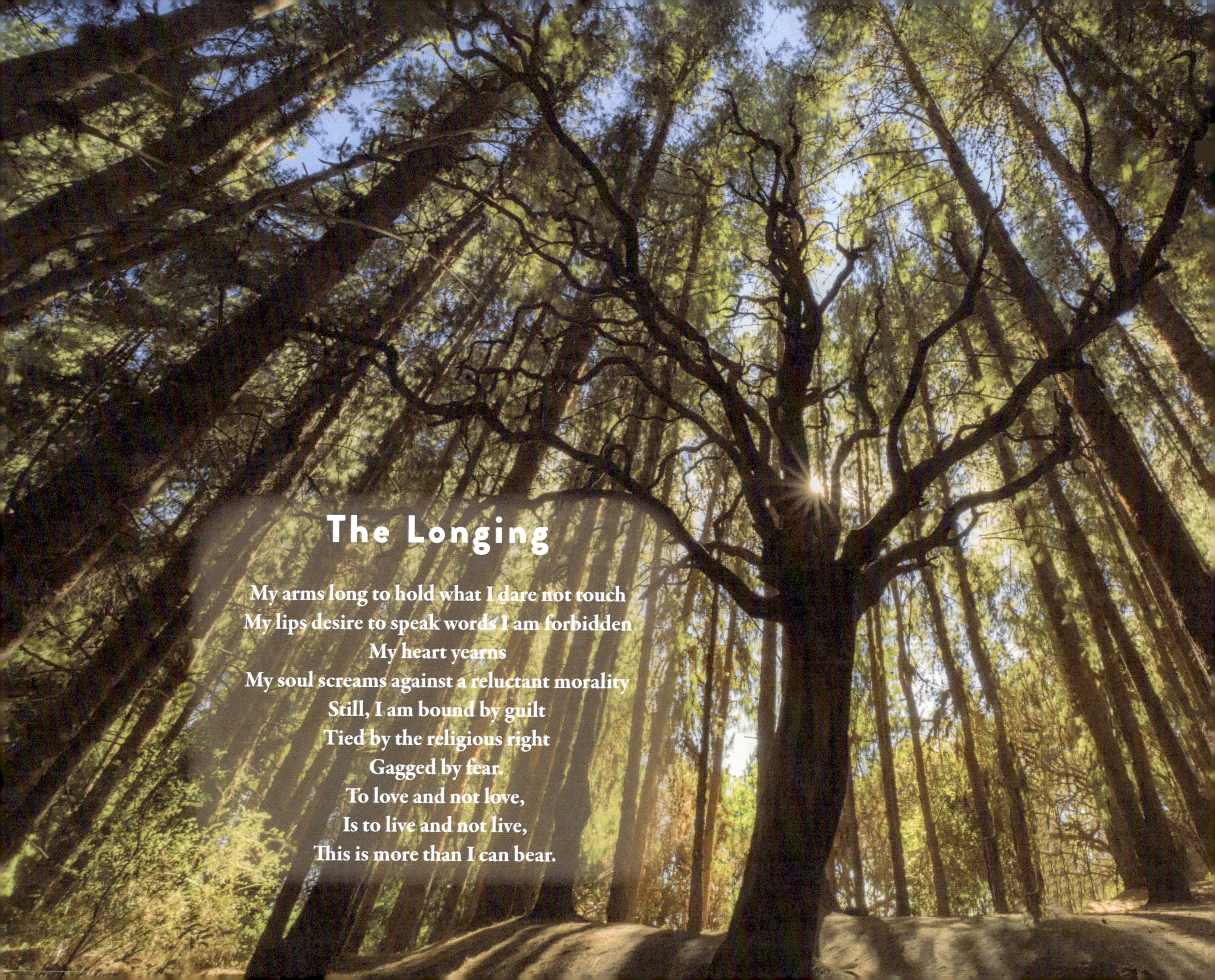

The Longing

My arms long to hold what I dare not touch
My lips desire to speak words I am forbidden
My heart yearns
My soul screams against a reluctant morality
Still, I am bound by guilt
Tied by the religious right
Gagged by fear.
To love and not love,
Is to live and not live,
This is more than I can bear.

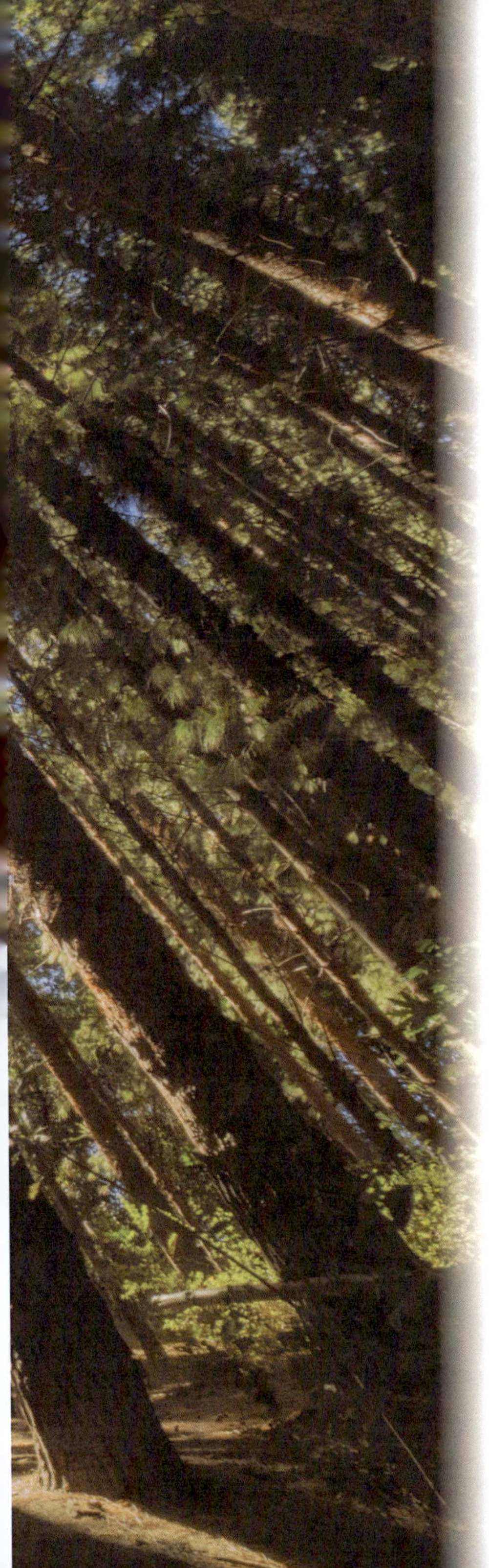

We've all met someone with whom we felt an immediate connection. Sometimes the timing is right and we are able to express that emotion, explore that connection, let those feelings blossom. You're floating on a cloud. Your heart is bursting with so much emotion, happiness, joy, lust, love, wonder, excitement, and hope. And then there are times when those feelings have to be denied.

Religion, morality, chivalry, even love, demand that you remain silent. But the heart knows no religion. The heart knows no moral code. The heart does not adhere to a higher code of conduct. The heart only feels.

When the heart meets another beating in harmony, it can only yearn for more. Our minds have been taught that it is immoral for a man to love another if he is married, or she is married, or both. But the heart cannot be taught so the mind struggles, and pulls to restrain the heart. The heart pains as it tugs against the chains, bruising itself against the bars of its prison cell. But the heart cannot be subdued.

The mind races with thoughts of all the terrible outcomes that could possibly befall him. The heart dreams of all the wonders that could be. The internal conflict tears at the very fabric of my soul.

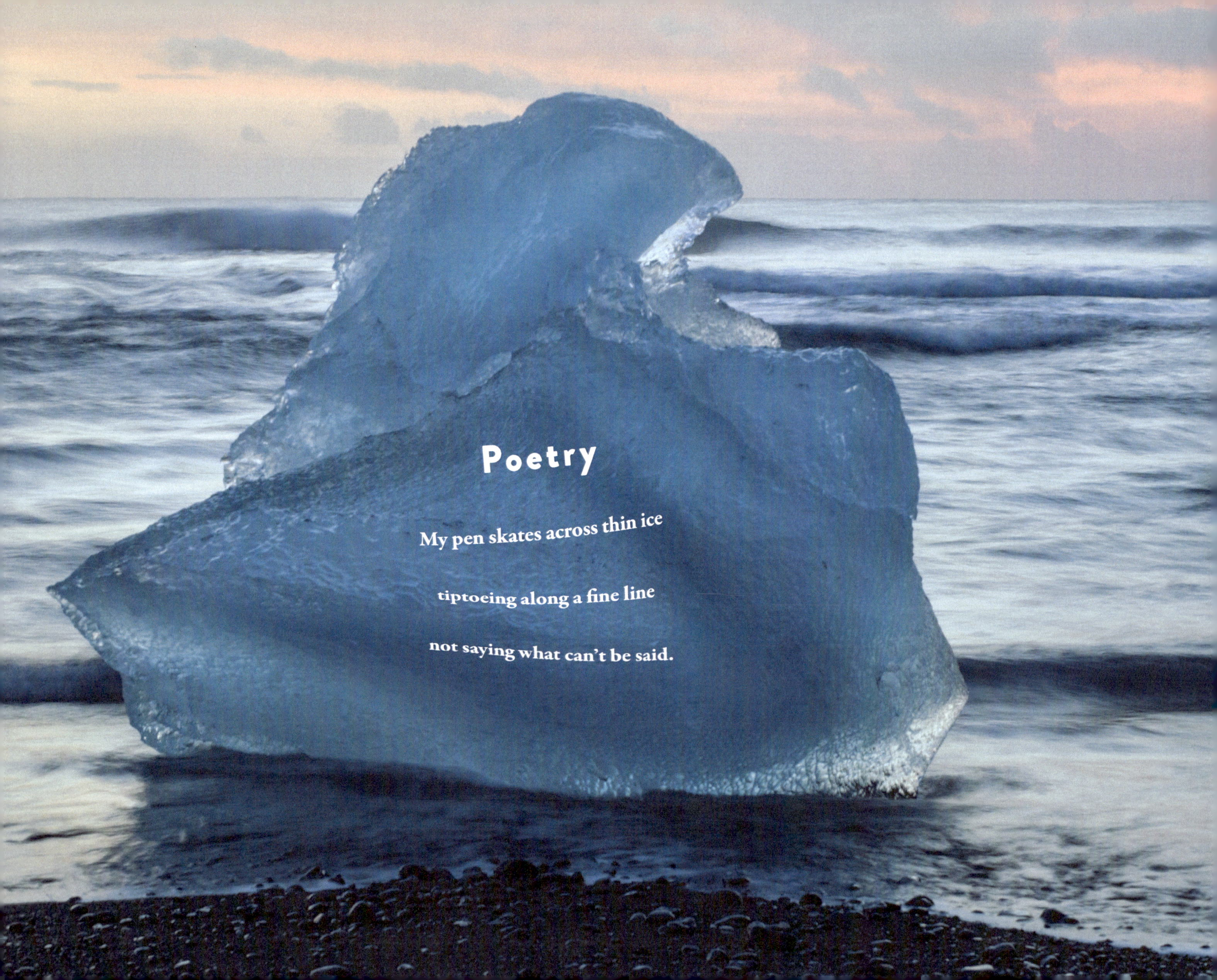
Poetry

My pen skates across thin ice

tiptoeing along a fine line

not saying what can't be said.

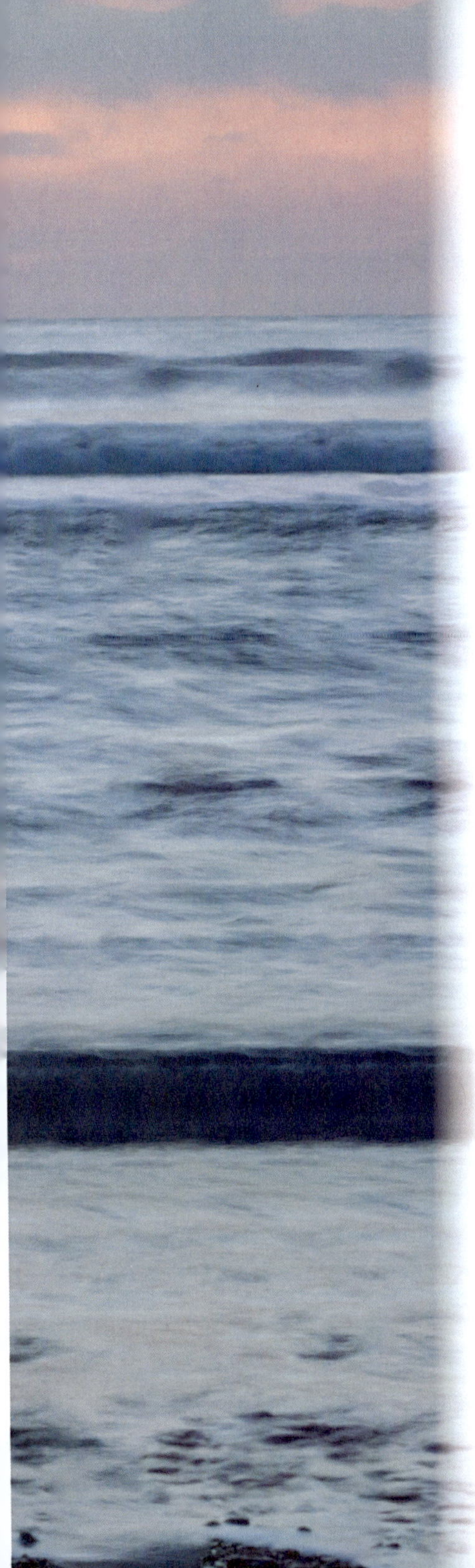

Whether it is love of another, nature, beauty, country or cause, poets select their words carefully. They speak their verse without hitting the topic head on. They say as much or more in the words they do not use as the ones they do. One false step could land them in hot water. One wrong word and all meaning is lost. To the suspicious wife a poem could be about a beautiful flower opening from bud to blossom, but to the muse the poem reveals feelings of desire and passion, longing and regret.

To openly confess my love to another would be to hurt one that I still love and loves me. So through poetry I don't say the words I'm not allowed to say. But my heart still sings.

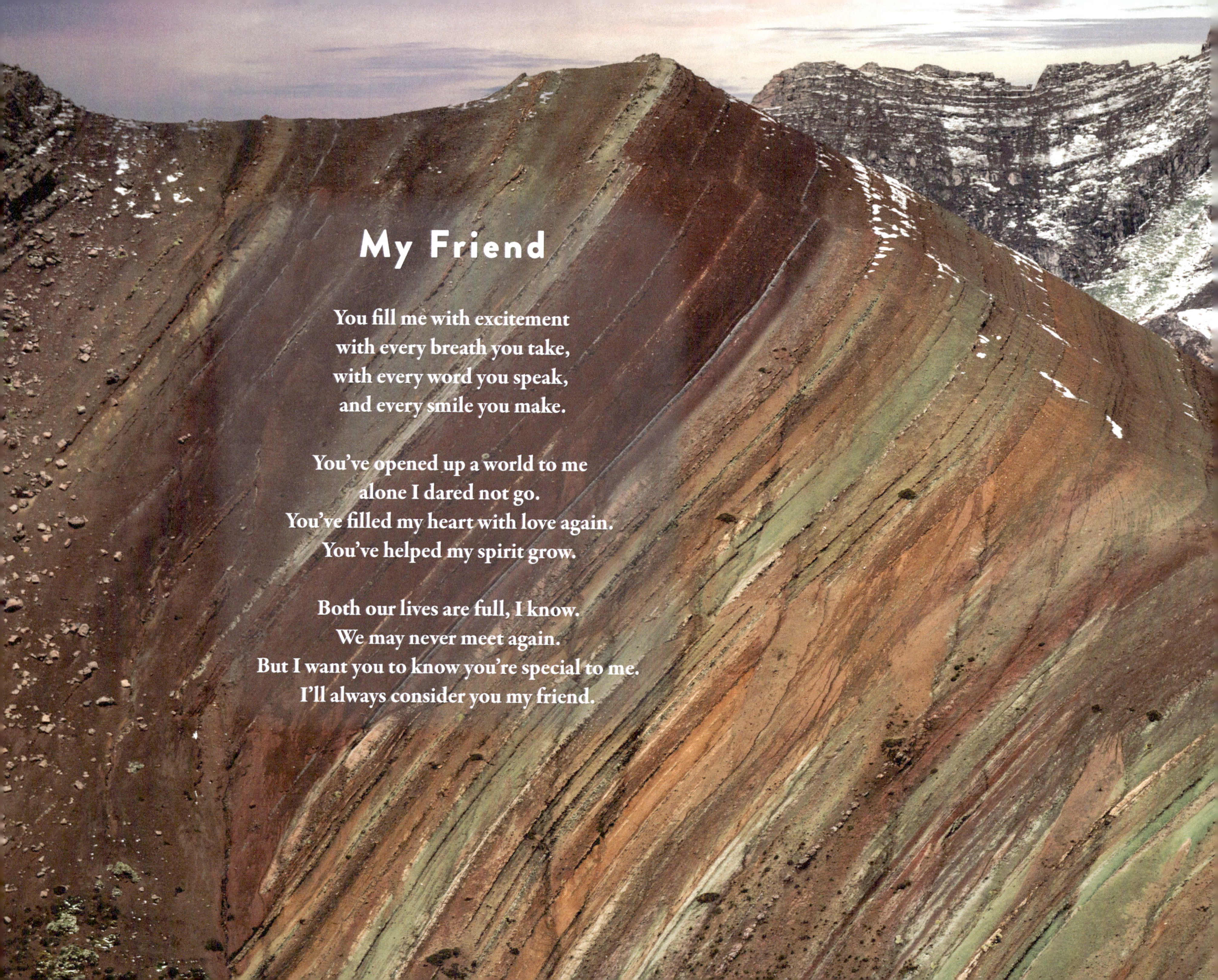

My Friend

You fill me with excitement
with every breath you take,
with every word you speak,
and every smile you make.

You've opened up a world to me
alone I dared not go.
You've filled my heart with love again.
You've helped my spirit grow.

Both our lives are full, I know.
We may never meet again.
But I want you to know you're special to me.
I'll always consider you my friend.

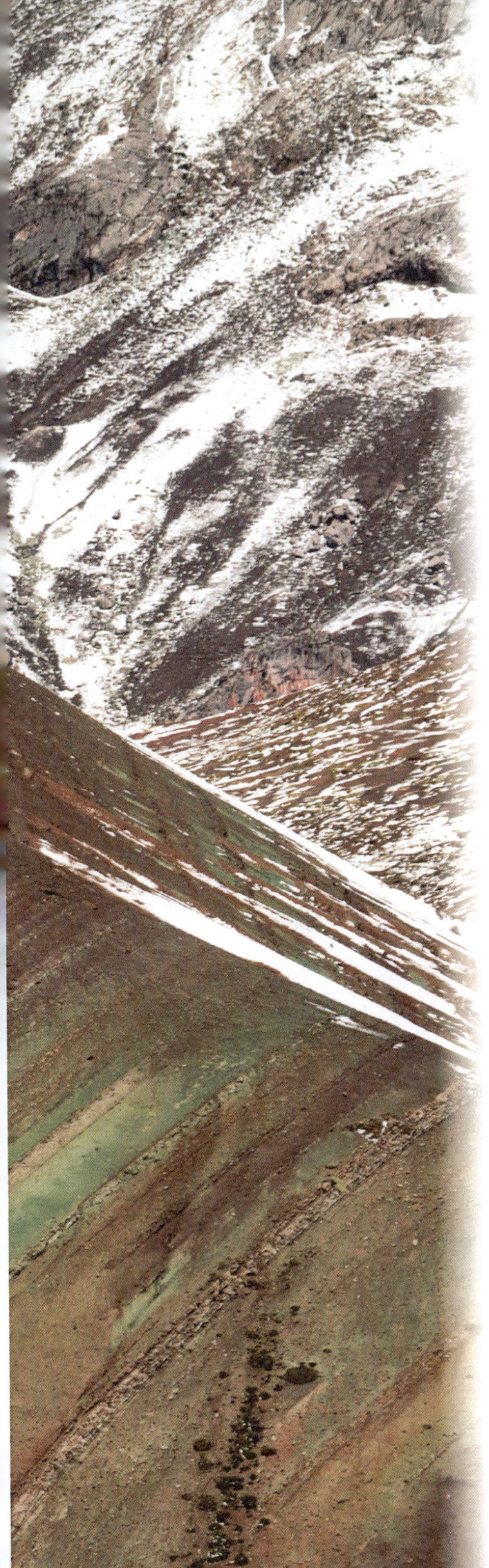

I've always loved poetry from a very young age. My favorite book as a child was Mother Goose Nursery Rhymes. I really liked the rhyme and meter and some of them were quite silly. As I grew I liked some of the classics like Milton, Frost, Whitman and others. I loved the movie Dead Poets Society. I also liked to write. I never had a love for English, and writing term papers or research papers was tiring, tedious work. But I liked to write short stories and would oftentimes write some for other kids in my class when they couldn't get their assignment done on time.

I wrote poetry too but not too much. Not until much later in life when I decided to go to college after the Marines and get my degree. There, I met my English Composition teacher and fell in love. I thought she was beautiful and through her I found my love of writing again. The love I felt for her wasn't the lusty type filled with carnal desire but one of deep admiration and appreciation for opening this world up to me again. A world where I can pour my pains onto the page and move on. A world where I can explore the meaning of my existence through unanswered questions, a world where my desires have no boundaries, a world that is safe and my thoughts stay my own until I'm ready to share them with others. A world where I can say everything I need to say.

You gave me this world and it's the greatest gift I've ever received. I will always hold you dear to my heart.

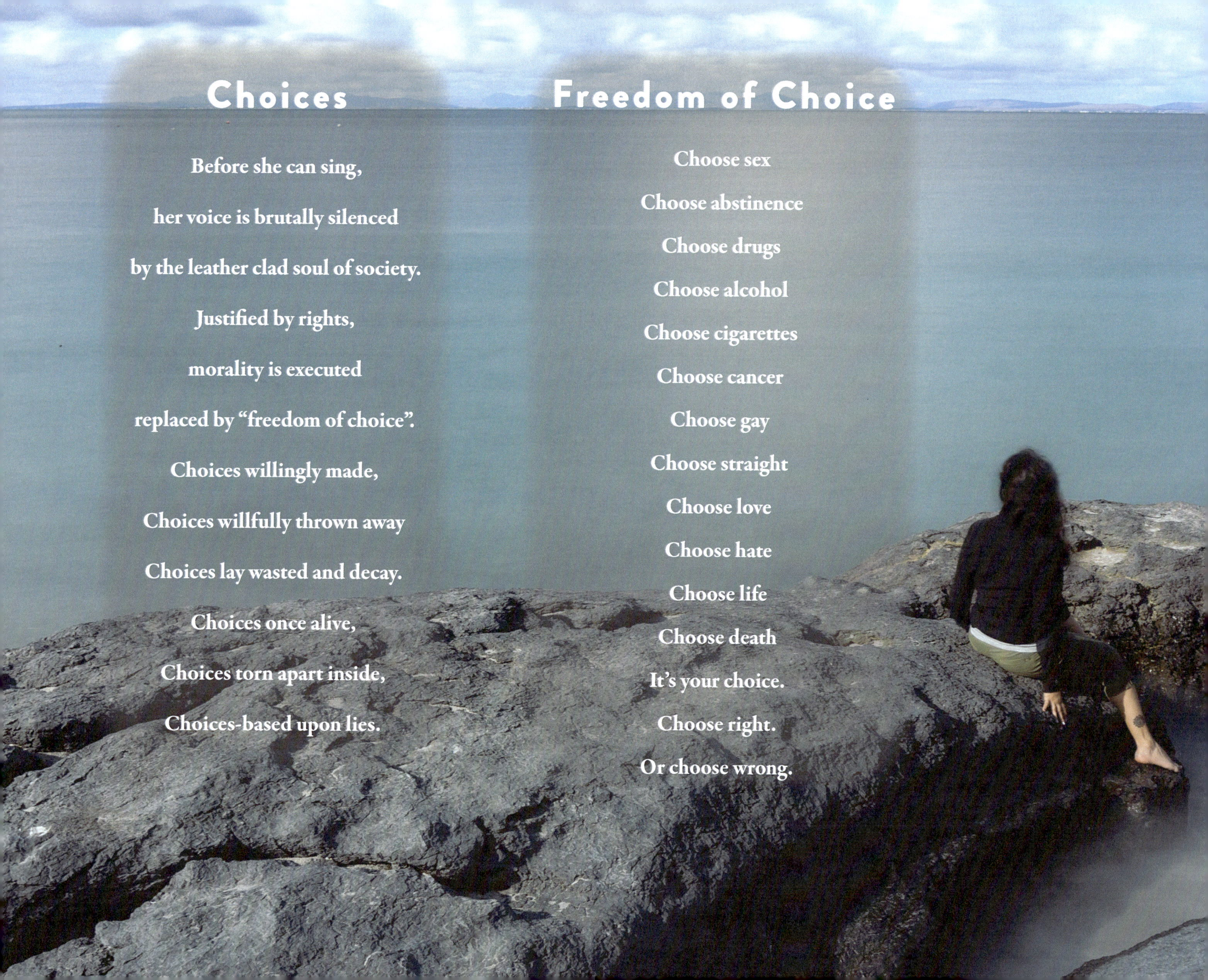

Choices

Before she can sing,

her voice is brutally silenced

by the leather clad soul of society.

Justified by rights,

morality is executed

replaced by "freedom of choice".

Choices willingly made,

Choices willfully thrown away

Choices lay wasted and decay.

Choices once alive,

Choices torn apart inside,

Choices-based upon lies.

Freedom of Choice

Choose sex

Choose abstinence

Choose drugs

Choose alcohol

Choose cigarettes

Choose cancer

Choose gay

Choose straight

Choose love

Choose hate

Choose life

Choose death

It's your choice.

Choose right.

Or choose wrong.

I grew up in Iowa in a fairly conservative family. Not very religious but we definitely didn't cater to any of those bleeding-heart liberal values. There was a great deal of political incorrectness and a certain amount of pride in that fact. So it just makes sense that as I grew up in the era of Regan and Republican influence that I too would become a conservative Republican. I joined the Marines right out of high school and promptly checked Catholic on the enlistment papers so I would get Sundays off during boot camp for mass. This was the beginning of my experience with religion. After boot camp I stopped going to church and led a raucous Marine Corps lifestyle until I met my first wife. There was a phase during my first marriage where we decided to take up religion. We gave it an honest effort. We went to bible study and even taught Sunday school. I took the commandments to heart.

I was faced with a situation while I was a young Marine where a friend asked for money to fund an abortion. Not being a religious type and caring deeply for this friend and her situation I sent her the money. It was only after finding religion that I felt a deep remorse for what I'd done. I know it wasn't my choice and if I didn't fund it someone else probably would have but I still had a part in it. Was it a boy, was it a girl, what would her name have been, where would she be now, what would she look like, who would she have become? I feel love and loss for the one I helped murder. It's a choice I made, she made, we made and it pains me to this day.

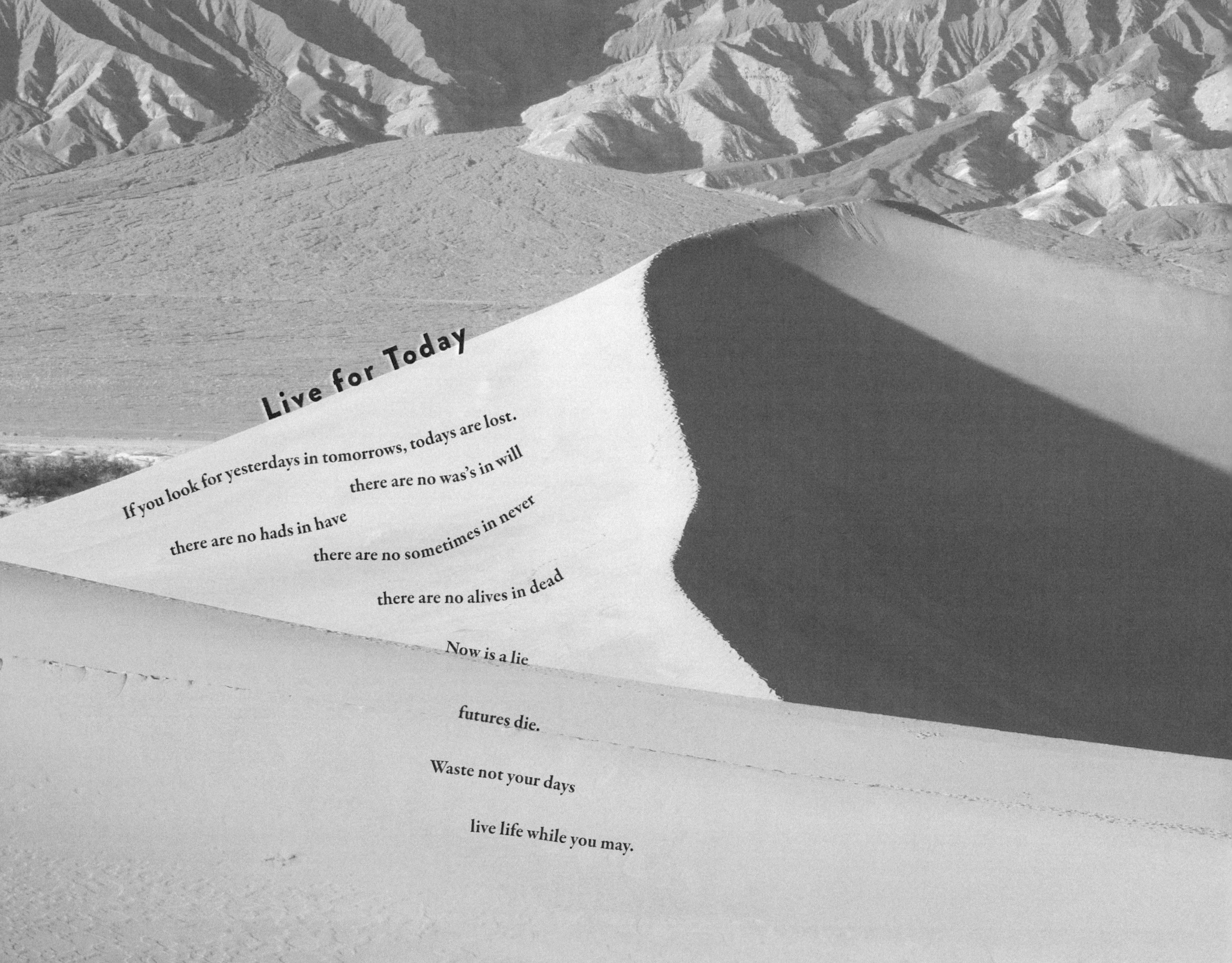

Live for Today

If you look for yesterdays in tomorrows, todays are lost.

there are no was's in will

there are no hads in have

there are no sometimes in never

there are no alives in dead

Now is a lie

futures die.

Waste not your days

live life while you may.

I went to church for a while and tried to live a life of faith but something didn't ring true to me. Some people are fine following with blind faith like sheep but I need logic, reason, and answers and too much of religion seemed like stuff they'd tell the ignorant masses to placate and control them. Is there a benefit for offering up your stresses to a higher power and unburdening yourself of your guilt? Definitely! Too much stress can kill you! So if you need to believe someone has magical powers given to them by the divine Lord above to absolve you of all your sins then go for it. But it's not for me.

The sins of this world are only sins if you define them as such. We are all human and human nature will cause you to do all sorts of things that upon reflection might not have been the best decision. We all have animal instincts especially when it comes to lust that are essential to the preservation of humanity. Is it healthy to sleep with everyone you feel sexually attracted to? No, but you can't deny the feelings exist. They are there and it's all part of being human. If we didn't have lusty thoughts for each other we may become extinct out of sheer boredom. Do we make mistakes? Do we sometimes act without thinking? Do we get so worked up that we rationalize bad decisions? Of course we do! But that is no reason to beat yourself up and there's no reason to hang onto that mistake the rest of your life. Live your life to the fullest and love every minute of it.

To my Love

(with a nod to Cummings)	(translated)
yIoCu beauty X (intelligence, love and passion).	I see in you beauty underscored by intelligence, love, and passion.
U m-desire-e	You fill me with desire
my heart/fire	my heart is on fire
let me feel me\you	let me feel me under you
me/you	me over you
ymoeu	me in you
comeme	come with me
quench my desire.	quench my desire.

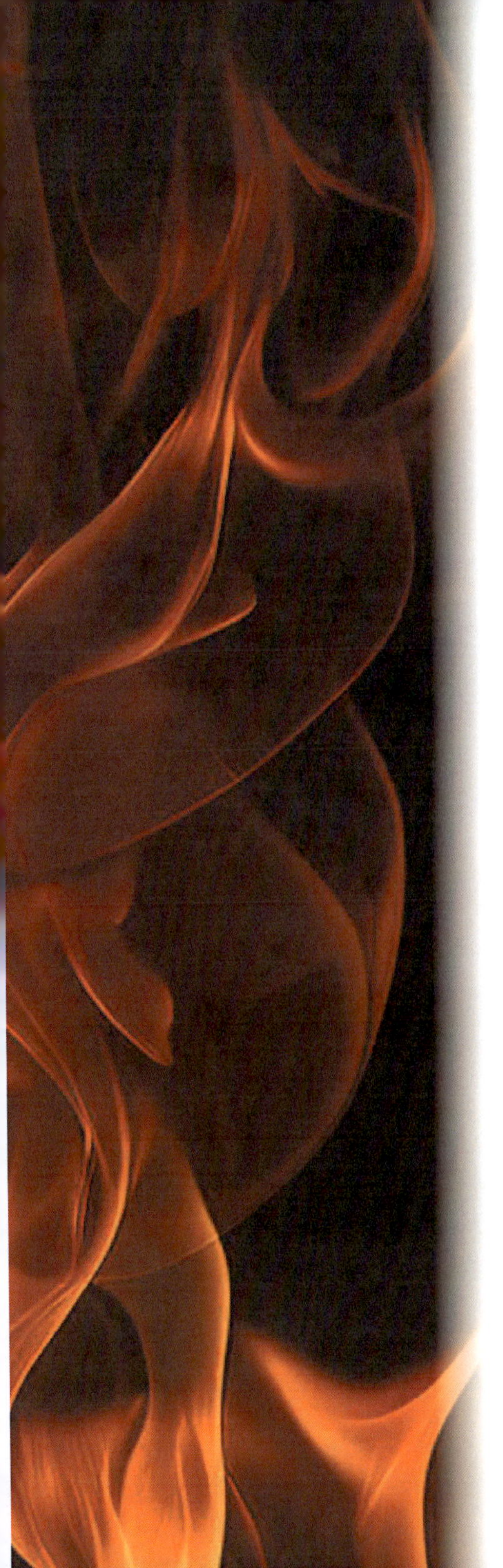

My studies brought me across a poem by EE Cummings titled The Anteater. I thought the use of the words to visually depict what he was saying was ingenious. Throughout the poem the words flowed back and forth like the tongue of the anteater scooping up the ants as they scurried across the page trying to escape. It really changed my perspective on writing poetry and added an extra dimension I was eager to explore. Not only is it possible to use the meanings of the words to convey thoughts, emotions, and scenery but the words themselves can add a physical, almost tangible, element bringing the vision to life and giving it motion as well as emotion.

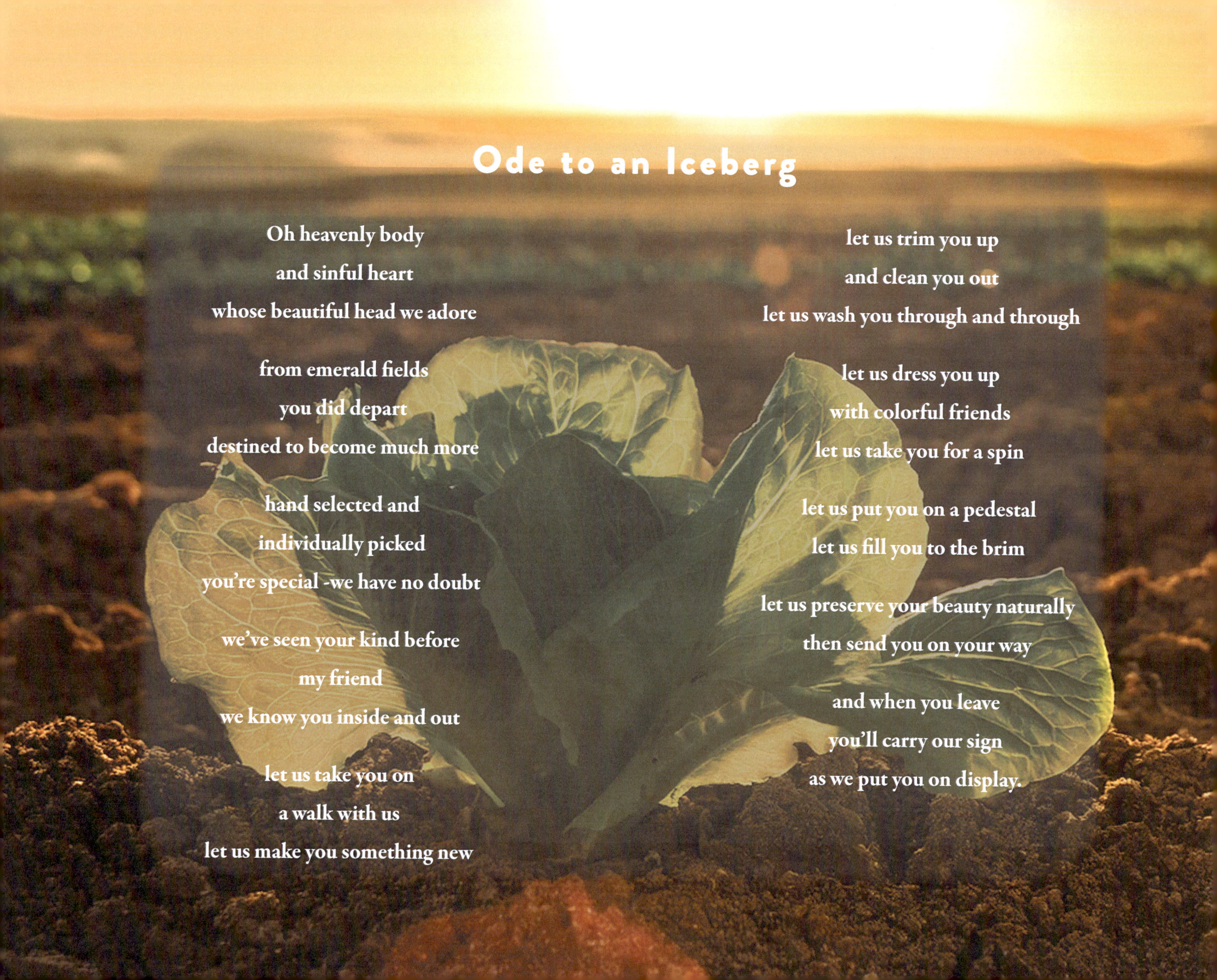

Ode to an Iceberg

Oh heavenly body
and sinful heart
whose beautiful head we adore

from emerald fields
you did depart
destined to become much more

hand selected and
individually picked
you're special -we have no doubt

we've seen your kind before
my friend
we know you inside and out

let us take you on
a walk with us
let us make you something new

let us trim you up
and clean you out
let us wash you through and through

let us dress you up
with colorful friends
let us take you for a spin

let us put you on a pedestal
let us fill you to the brim

let us preserve your beauty naturally
then send you on your way

and when you leave
you'll carry our sign
as we put you on display.

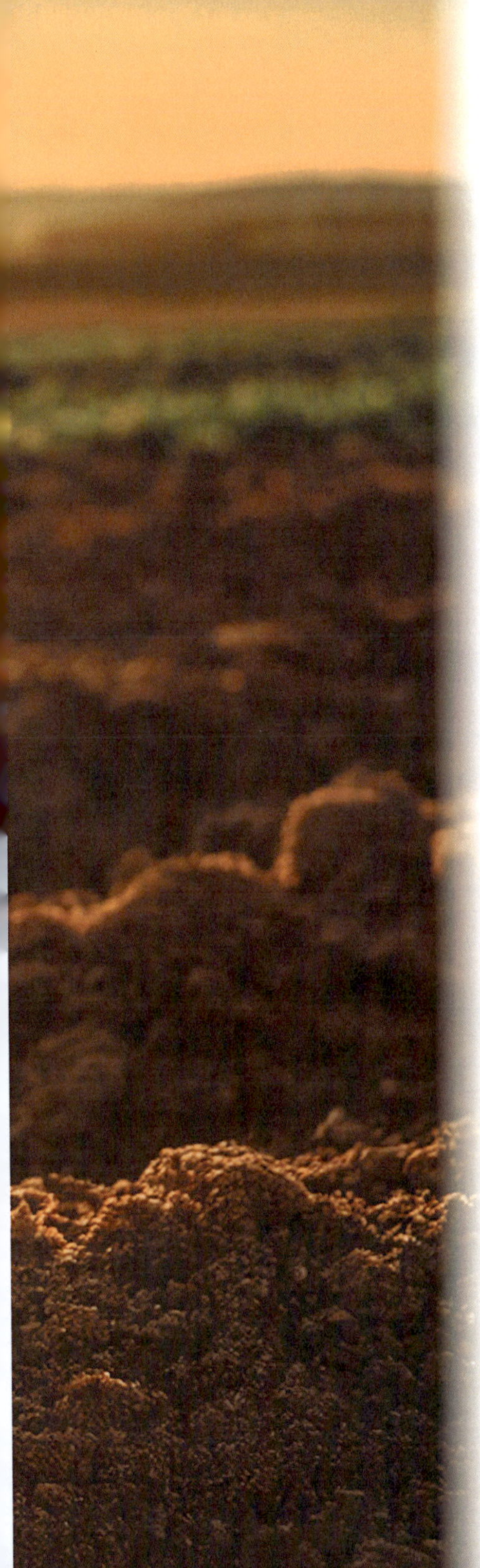

How to make bagged salad:

Pick

Trim *(remove outer leaves and core)*

Cut

Mix with carrots and purple cabbage

Wash

Spin Dry

Package *(remove oxygen to preserve)*

Ship

Have you ever wondered what it would be like to write a poem about your work? Well one day I was playing around and I pictured myself picking up a head of iceberg lettuce much like Hamlet picking up the skull of his dead father and waxing poetic. I worked for a company that made bagged salad for eight and a half years and maybe it was getting to me or maybe I developed a deep love of salad, but as iceberg lettuce was the main ingredient to our classic salad this one goes out to it.

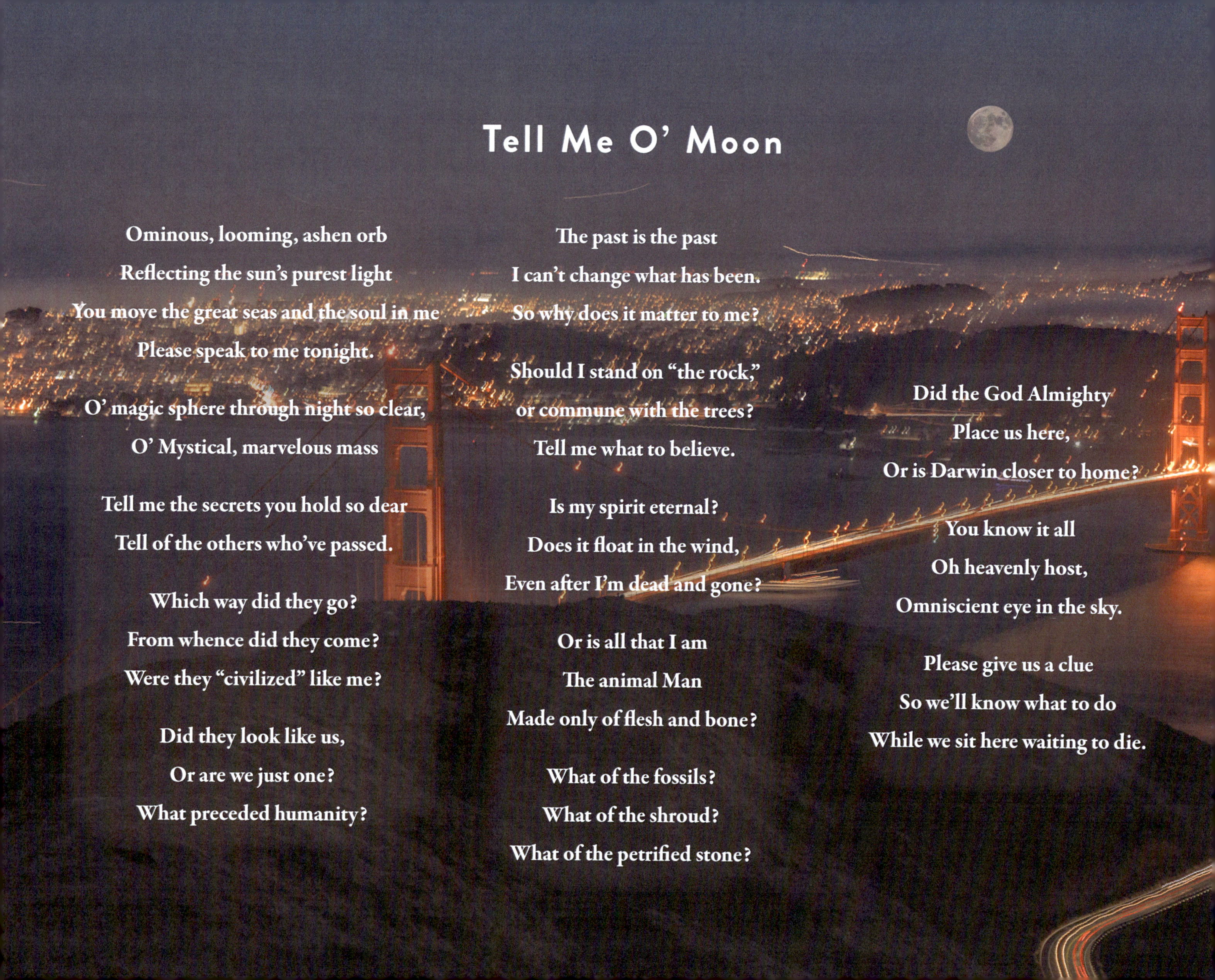

Tell Me O' Moon

Ominous, looming, ashen orb
Reflecting the sun's purest light
You move the great seas and the soul in me
Please speak to me tonight.

O' magic sphere through night so clear,
O' Mystical, marvelous mass

Tell me the secrets you hold so dear
Tell of the others who've passed.

Which way did they go?
From whence did they come?
Were they "civilized" like me?

Did they look like us,
Or are we just one?
What preceded humanity?

The past is the past
I can't change what has been.
So why does it matter to me?

Should I stand on "the rock,"
or commune with the trees?
Tell me what to believe.

Is my spirit eternal?
Does it float in the wind,
Even after I'm dead and gone?

Or is all that I am
The animal Man
Made only of flesh and bone?

What of the fossils?
What of the shroud?
What of the petrified stone?

Did the God Almighty
Place us here,
Or is Darwin closer to home?

You know it all
Oh heavenly host,
Omniscient eye in the sky.

Please give us a clue
So we'll know what to do
While we sit here waiting to die.

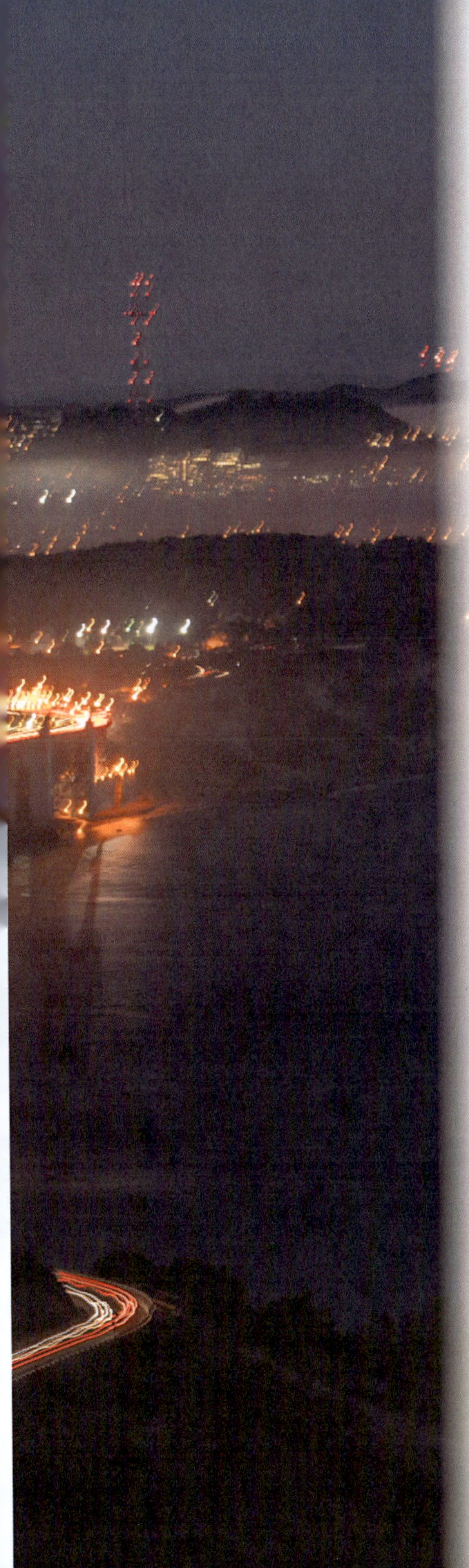

Throughout man's existence we've been obsessed with the meaning of life. It is hard to believe that we aren't meant for some higher purpose. Why would we be given the ability to invent and create the things we've made, or the ability to reason, to understand our own mortality (to the extent that we do), or the ability to continuously learn something new, or to love, or feel loss?

Why we're here and where we're going has a great deal to do with our perspective of how human life began on this planet. If we believe we were created by God and the bible has a fairly definite timeline of when that happened, then how do we explain the fossil records that go back well before God created life? There weren't any dinosaurs on Noah's ark or anywhere in the bible. If you believe man evolved from single-cell organisms then where is the fossilized evidence of the evolutionary process?

How were the planets formed? Who has the answers? There is someone who saw it all, if only they could only tell us we'd know what to do.

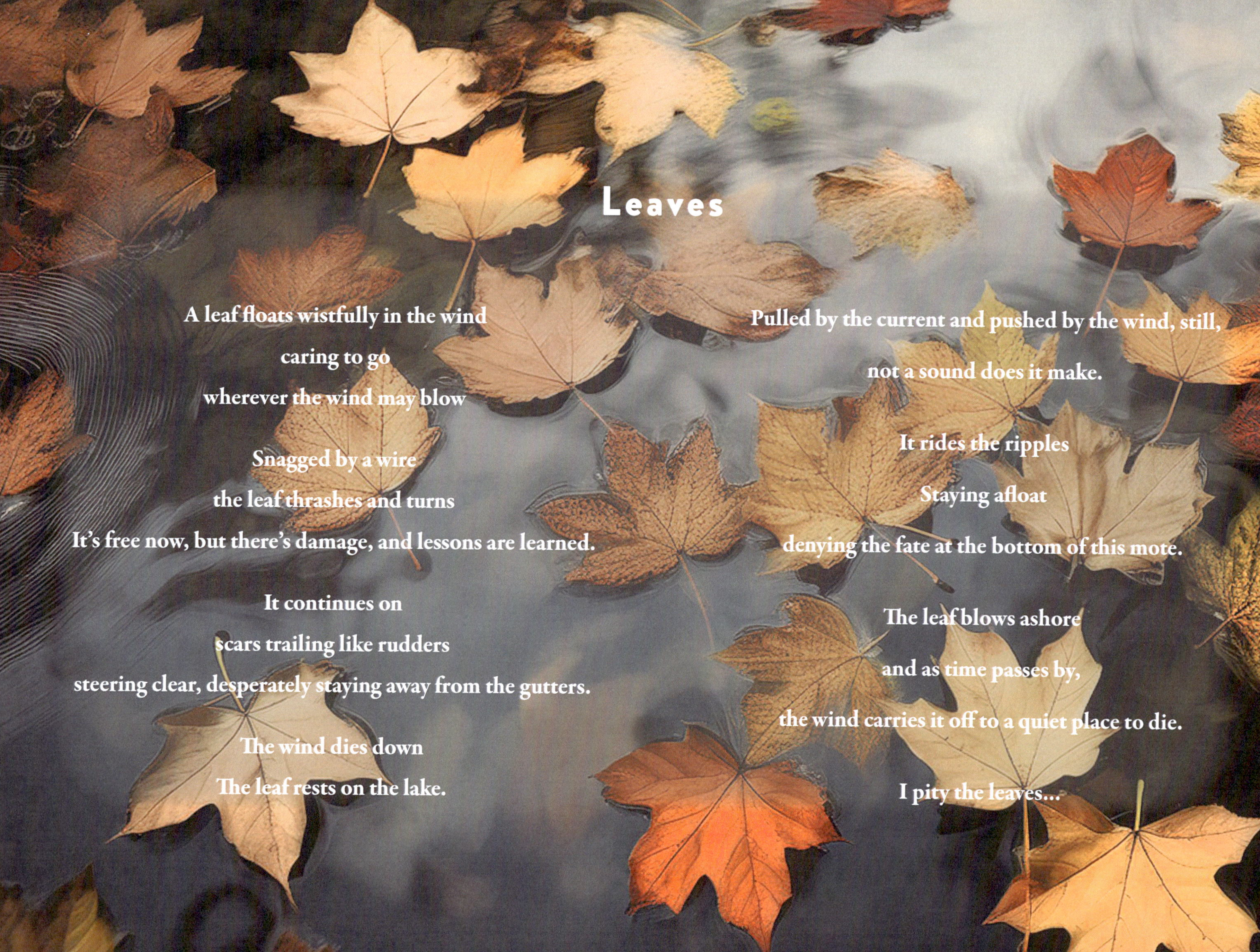

Leaves

A leaf floats wistfully in the wind
caring to go
wherever the wind may blow

Snagged by a wire
the leaf thrashes and turns
It's free now, but there's damage, and lessons are learned.

It continues on
scars trailing like rudders
steering clear, desperately staying away from the gutters.

The wind dies down
The leaf rests on the lake.

Pulled by the current and pushed by the wind, still,
not a sound does it make.

It rides the ripples

Staying afloat

denying the fate at the bottom of this mote.

The leaf blows ashore

and as time passes by,

the wind carries it off to a quiet place to die.

I pity the leaves...

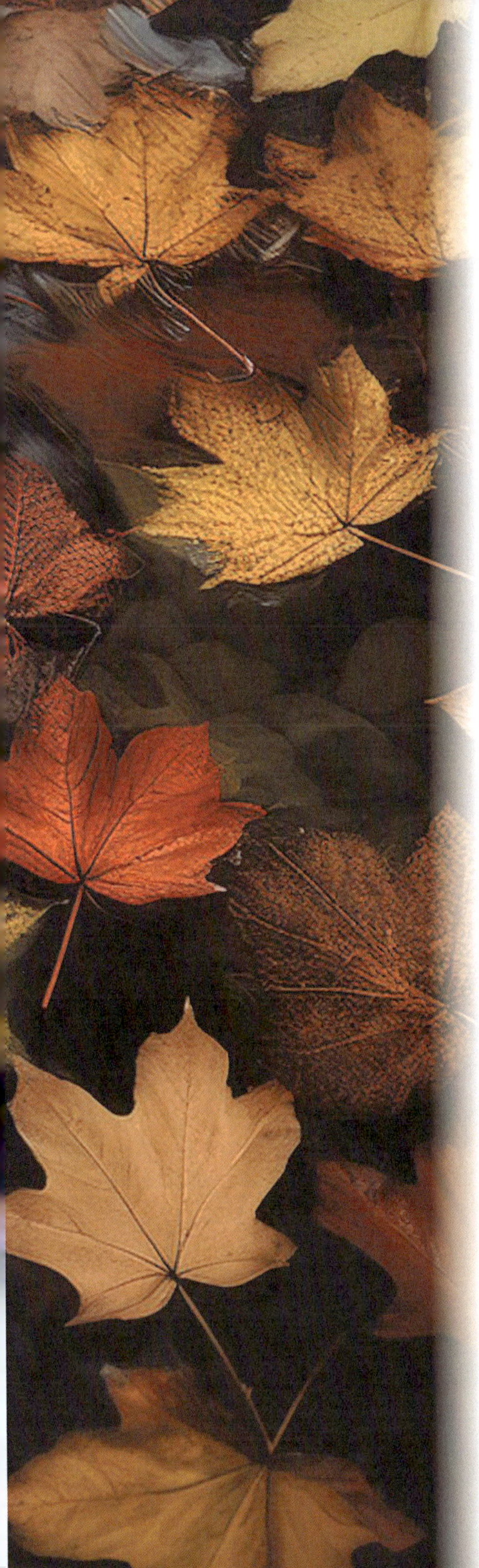

We've all known people who just seem to drift through life aimlessly wandering whichever way the wind blows. And sometimes we ourselves feel like the ones being tossed by the great unseen forces around us. Sometimes it's smooth sailing and we make it through the turbulent times with hardly a scratch, other times we end up drowning under the weight of the world and our own sorrows and sometimes we end up broken and scarred living on the streets.

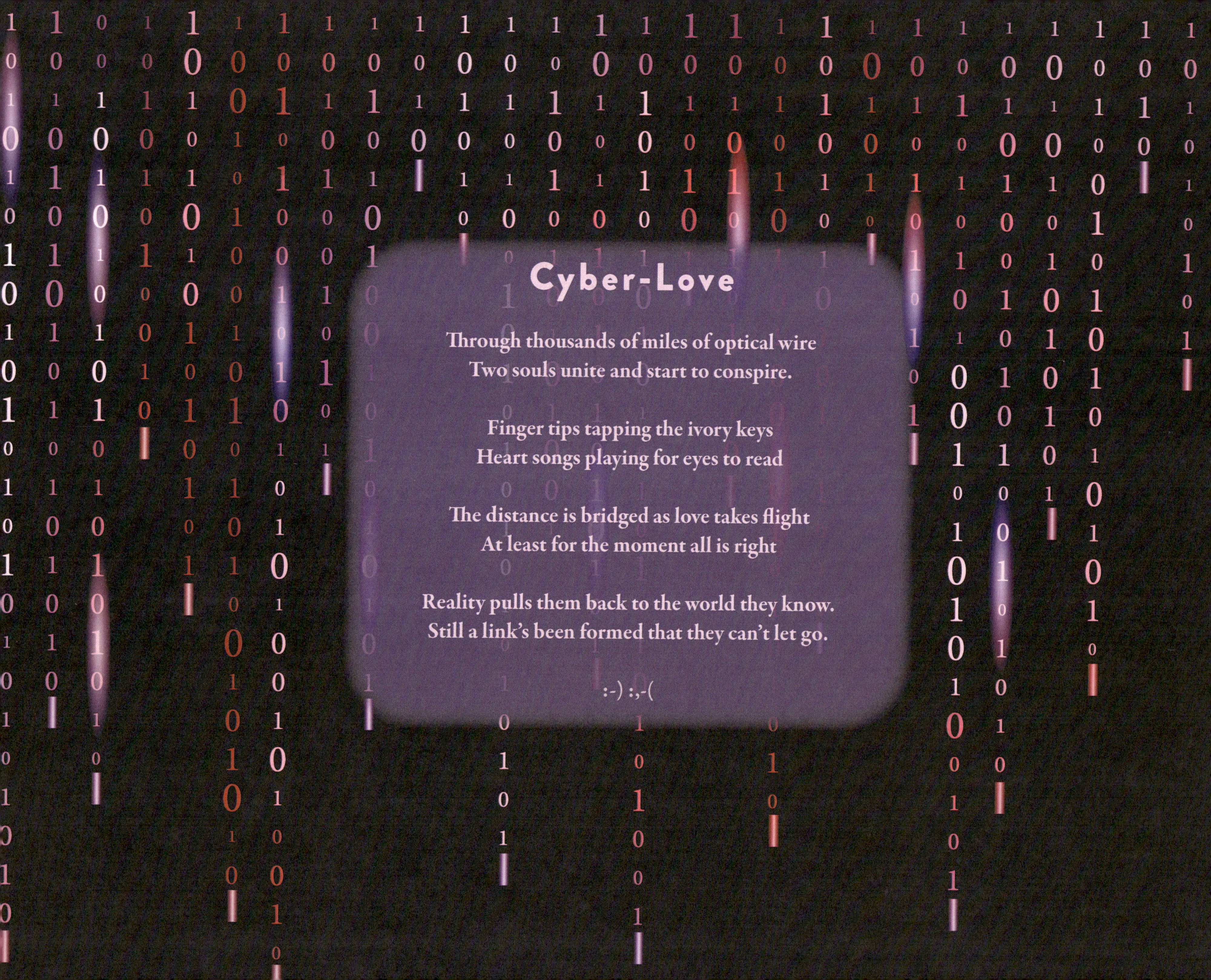

Cyber-Love

Through thousands of miles of optical wire
Two souls unite and start to conspire.

Finger tips tapping the ivory keys
Heart songs playing for eyes to read

The distance is bridged as love takes flight
At least for the moment all is right

Reality pulls them back to the world they know.
Still a link's been formed that they can't let go.

:-) :,-(

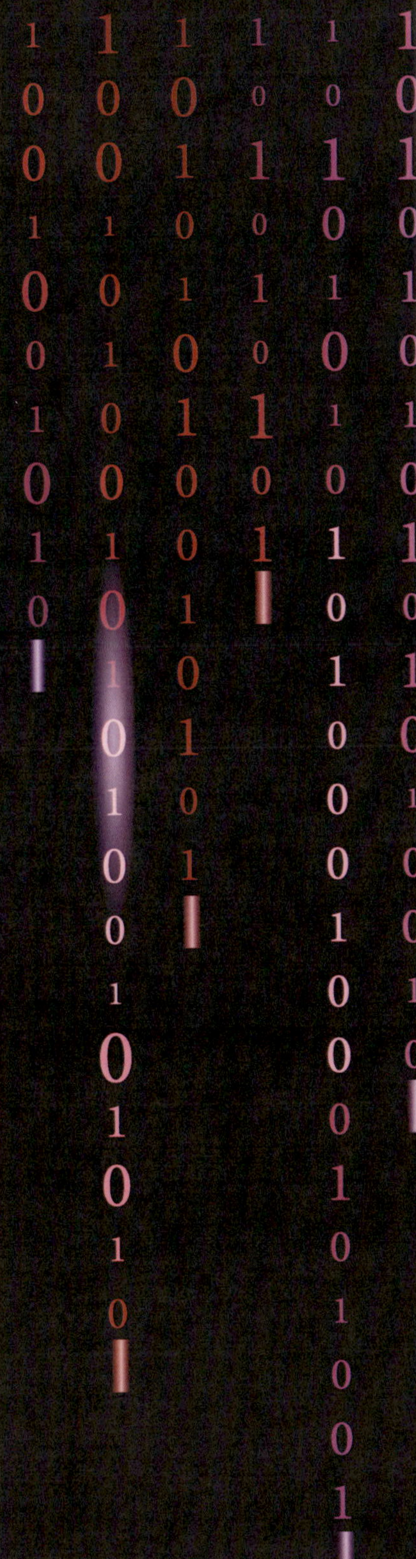

In the age of the internet meeting people has become much easier. You can hide behind a screen and only show the other person the ideal part of you. The person you want to be. The middle-aged man is now his youthful twenty-something self still full of idealism and lust for life, not encumbered by the pressures of life, work, failed relationships, poor health or any other unattractive qualities. He is a rock-star talking to the supermodel at the other end of the wire. All the possibilities are out there. The

fantasy becomes a reality and he feels alive again. For the moment.

My Fantasy

Through the darkest reaches of my mind
your spirit calls out to me,
descending from crystalline mountains
to the deep, clear blue sea.

Wading through misty memories your essence stirs my soul
As the world melts into nothingness and unconsciousness takes hold.

I see you coming through the mist, gown clinging in the breeze
Hair gently flowing around your face, eyes consuming me.
The mist caresses your tender skin, droplets hug your cheek,
I yearn to taste those parting lips…
You are my fantasy.

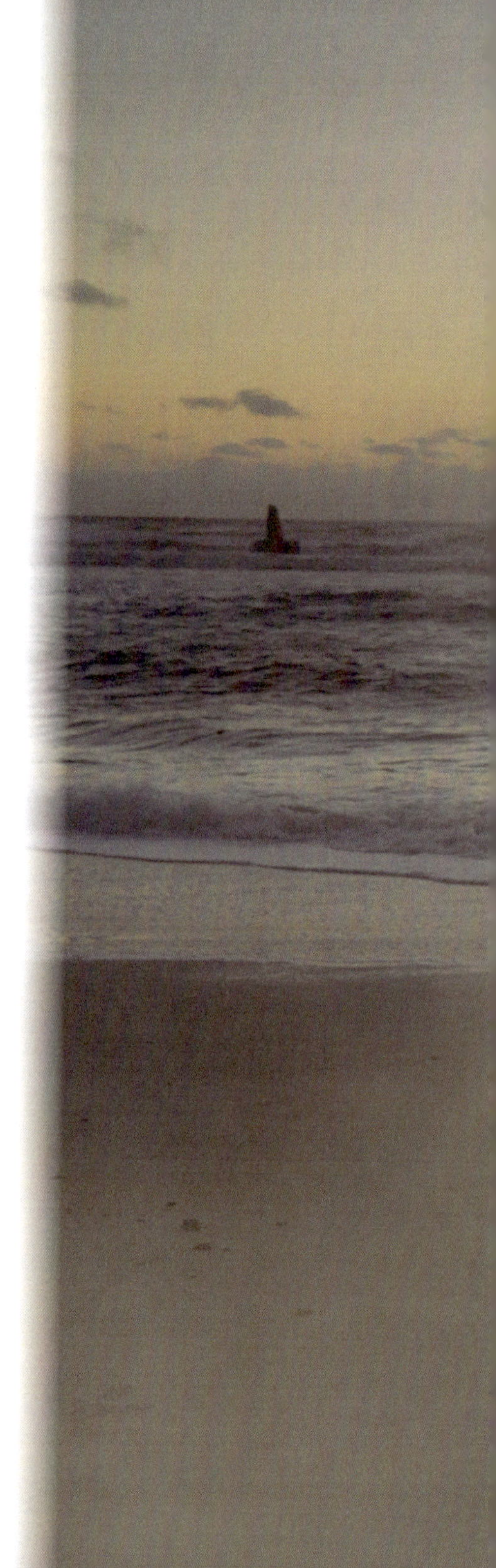

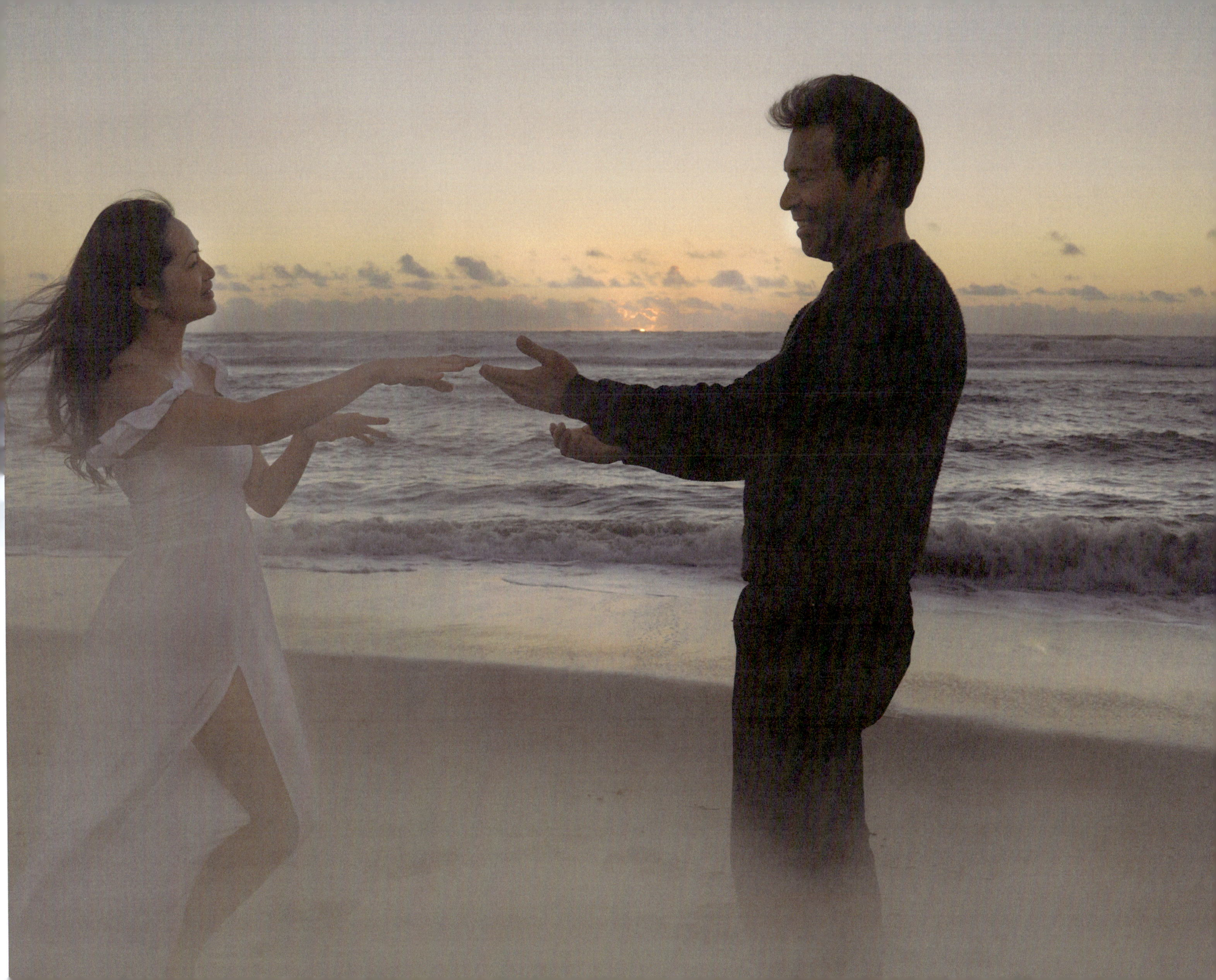

The Wall

A mason builds a wall,
to protect his humble home.
Working hard both night and day,
until the job is done.

It's only a minimal wall,
at this time he would agree.
Meant to keep out villains,
and wild animals, you see.

It does its job remarkably,
for a while, anyway.
'Till a cunning wolf jumps the wall
and steals a sheep away.

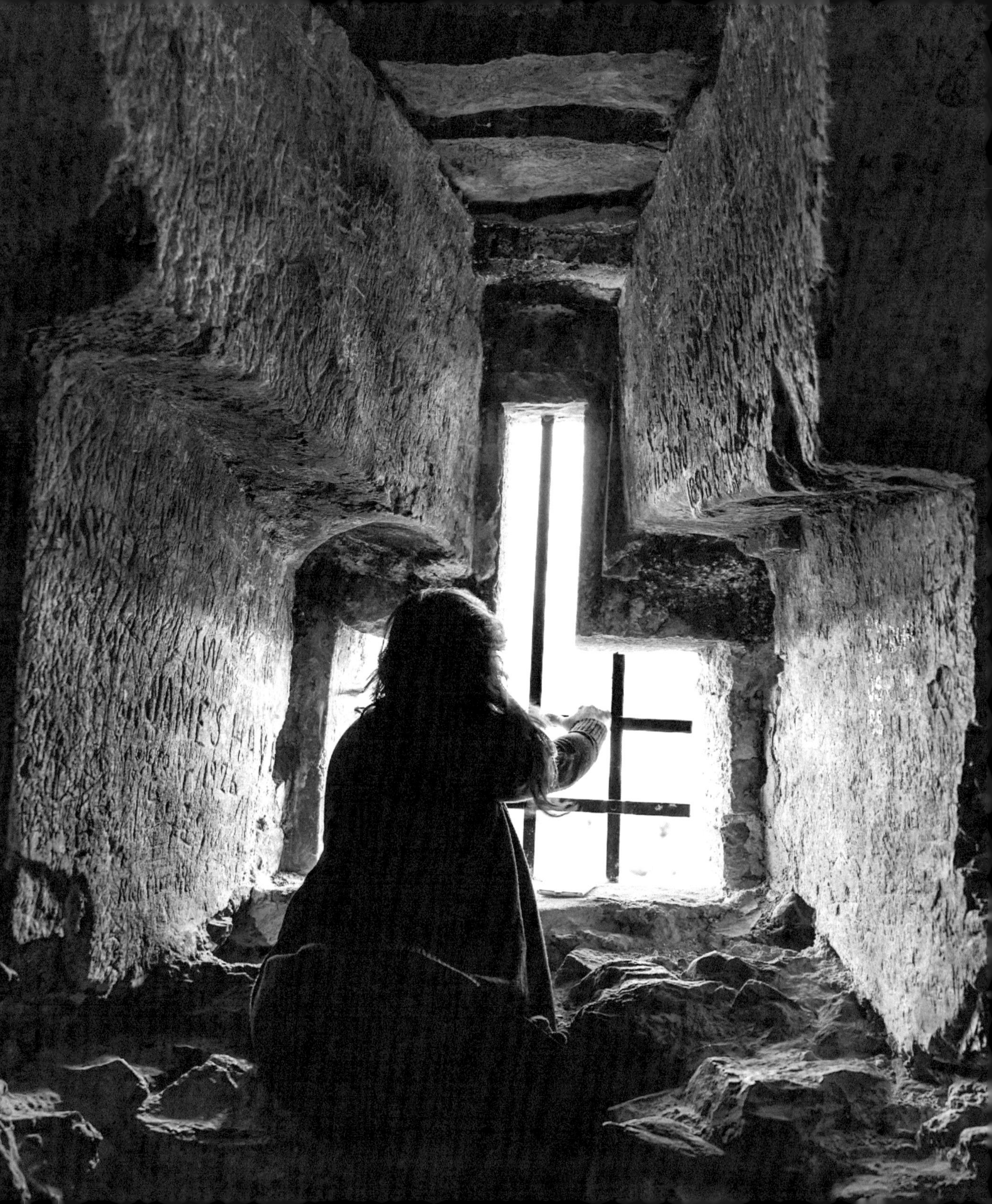

The mason mends his broken home
after tearful days of work.
Then sets to building the wall,
ten times higher than the first.

The beasts denied,
his house is safe,
the wall's a great success!

But the mason soon dies
for he's trapped himself in,
denying his love to the rest.

Every time our heart breaks we try to protect ourselves from suffering the same pain again. Each time it hurts more and lasts longer. When we love someone who's been hurt by others before or by us, all we want to do is find a way to tear down the wall. We want to show them we're different. We want to comfort and protect them and give them the love they need to feel whole again. But sometimes the hurt is so bad there is no way in. Or out.

The Dream

Eyes of green and jet black hair
As she enters the room I can't help but stare
Poetry in motion, a beauty refined
A dream I've dreamt a million times

The first time my eyes beheld her face
I was taken back to a familiar place
We've met before on another plane
Somewhere in time, some other frame

Pictures flash, smiles unite
Eyes to eyes, but out of sight.
The mind is reeling to place the place
Where once before I'd seen her face.

Then dreams rewind to an ocean scene
Cool waves are crashing next to me
Hand in hand we'd walked the shore
In dreams I've dreamt those times before.

A heartbeat skipped for what seems a lifetime
As the memories rush forward and back in time

And reality seems so far away,
As footsteps tread lightly on air these days,

But reality sinks her bitter teeth
Into the dreamy scene.

And the harsh light of day reveals to me
Her love could never be.

Timing is everything I've said in the past
As I find myself restrained
So I shall wait and hope once more
To wake in the dream I've dreamt before.

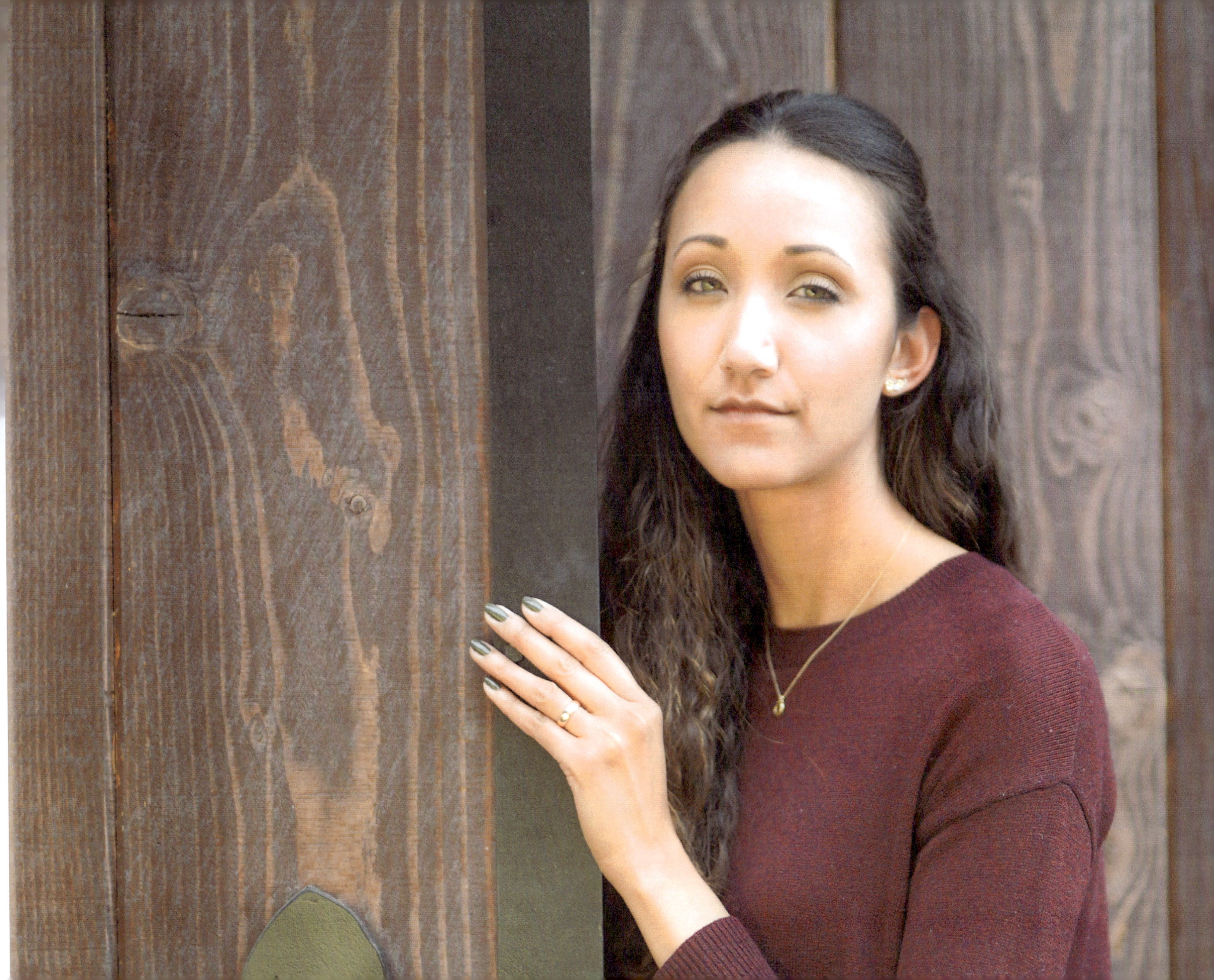

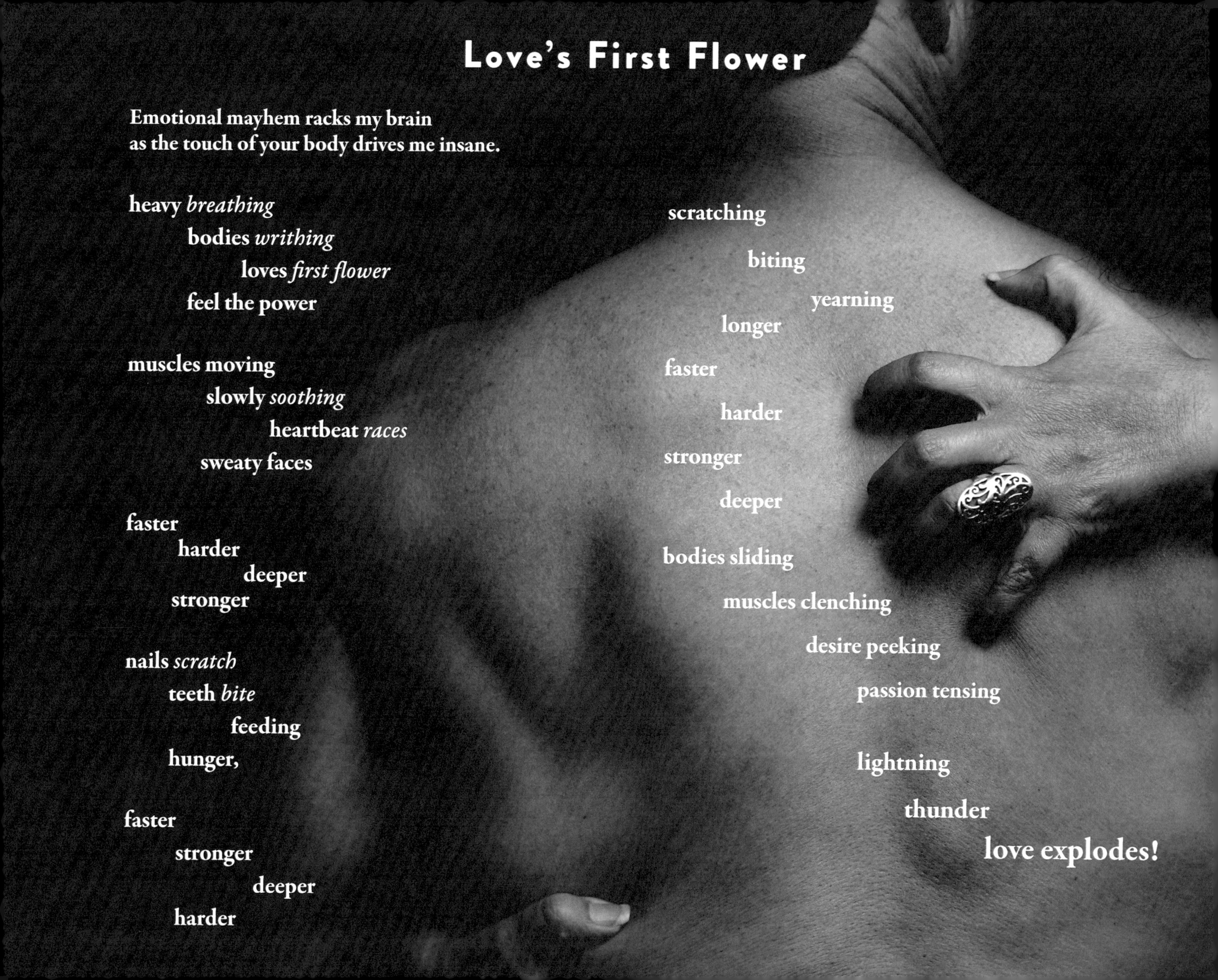

Love's First Flower

Emotional mayhem racks my brain
as the touch of your body drives me insane.

heavy *breathing*
   bodies *writhing*
      loves *first flower*
  feel the power

muscles moving
   slowly *soothing*
      heartbeat *races*
  sweaty faces

faster
  harder
    deeper
  stronger

nails *scratch*
  teeth *bite*
   feeding
  hunger,

faster
  stronger
    deeper
  harder

scratching
   biting
     yearning
    longer
  faster
   harder
  stronger
   deeper

bodies sliding
   muscles clenching
    desire peeking
     passion tensing

     lightning
      thunder
       love explodes!

warm

waves

crash

over

us

and

drowns

our

souls.

softly

so sweet...

gently

heartbeats slow

warm salty kisses on lips and nose

cheek brushes cheek

so soft...

I hold you in my arms,
we drift off to sleep.

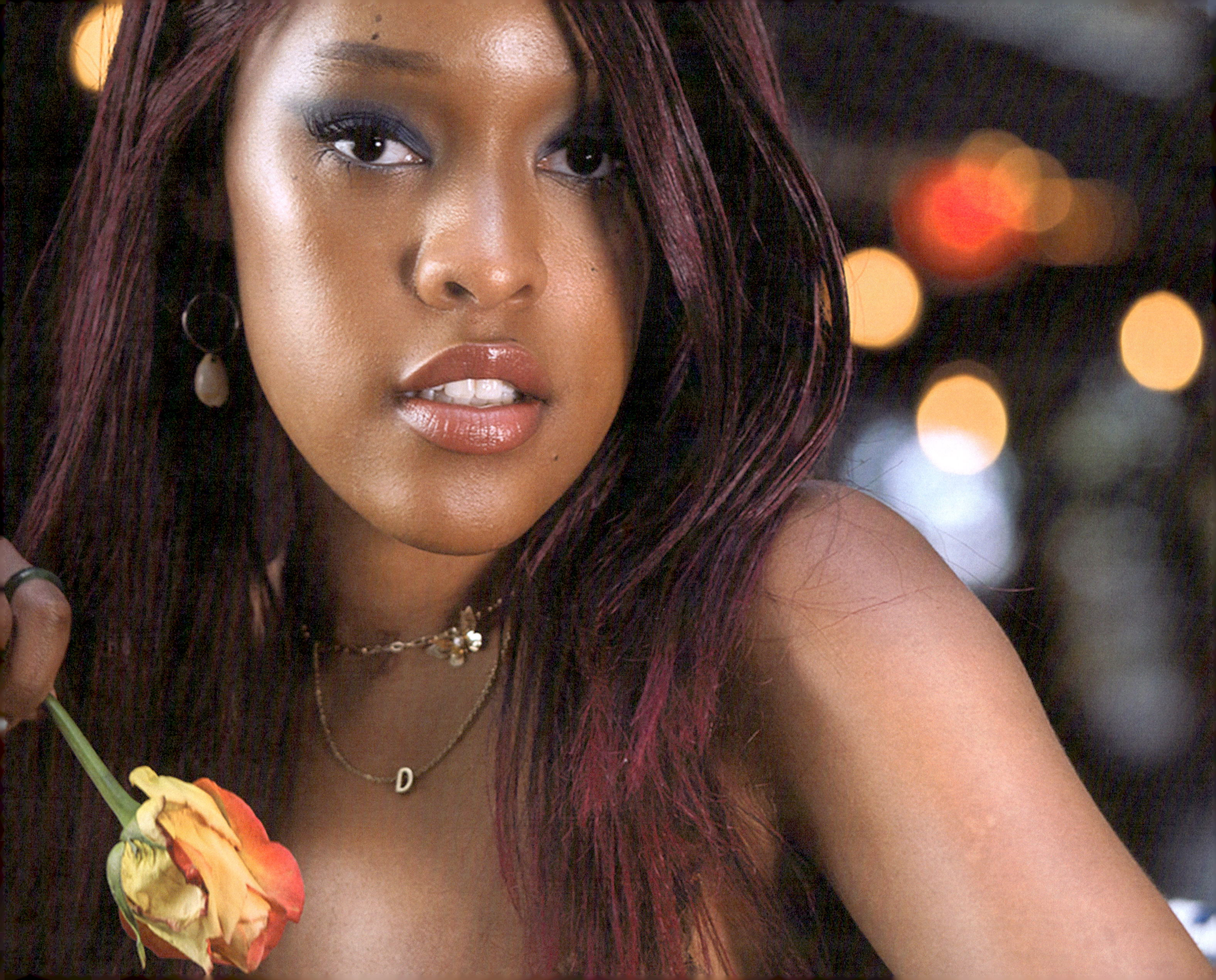

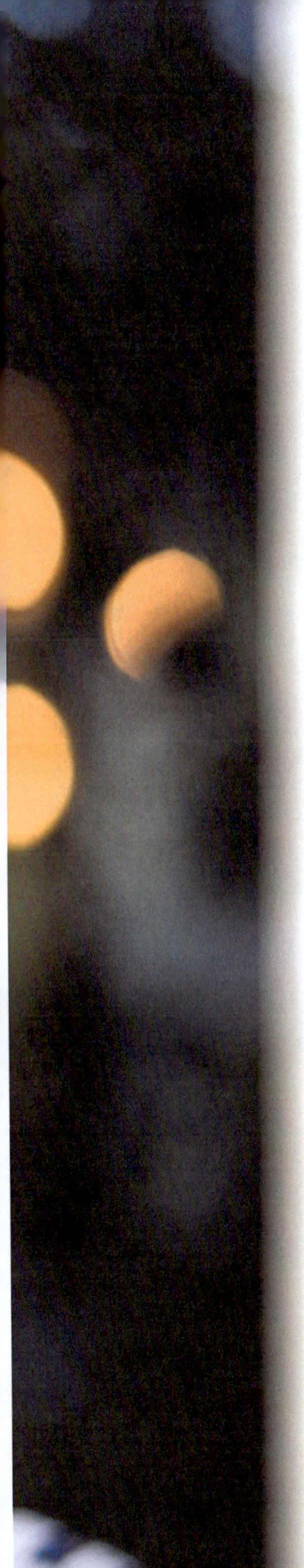

The Rose

A daisy is a weed until it blooms.
A rose is just a thorn.
For the love of a weed there is a drought
for the love of a rose a storm

I've seen the rose you hide inside
sheltered from my rain.
But without my love it will surely die
and cause my heart such pain.

Don't hide from me your precious bloom
let me smell it's fragrant air.
Let me hold it in my gentle hands
And in my loving stare.

Let me feed your rose with my sweet love
Let me tend it for a while.
Let me teach your rose to bloom again
and make your heart to smile.

Setting Love Free

He who says he loves everything
speaks hypocritical lies.
He who says he loves nothing,
a lonely fool does die.

He who says he loves only one,
to the one he loves, he lies.
For love is an endless, boundless stream,
touching countless lives.

I let go of my jealous possessiveness
that binds you in your gloom.
Feel free to show your love for me,
Or whomever you may choose.

I know your love for me is true
but I've smothered it with pride.
I've chained your spirit to my soul
and turned you cold inside.

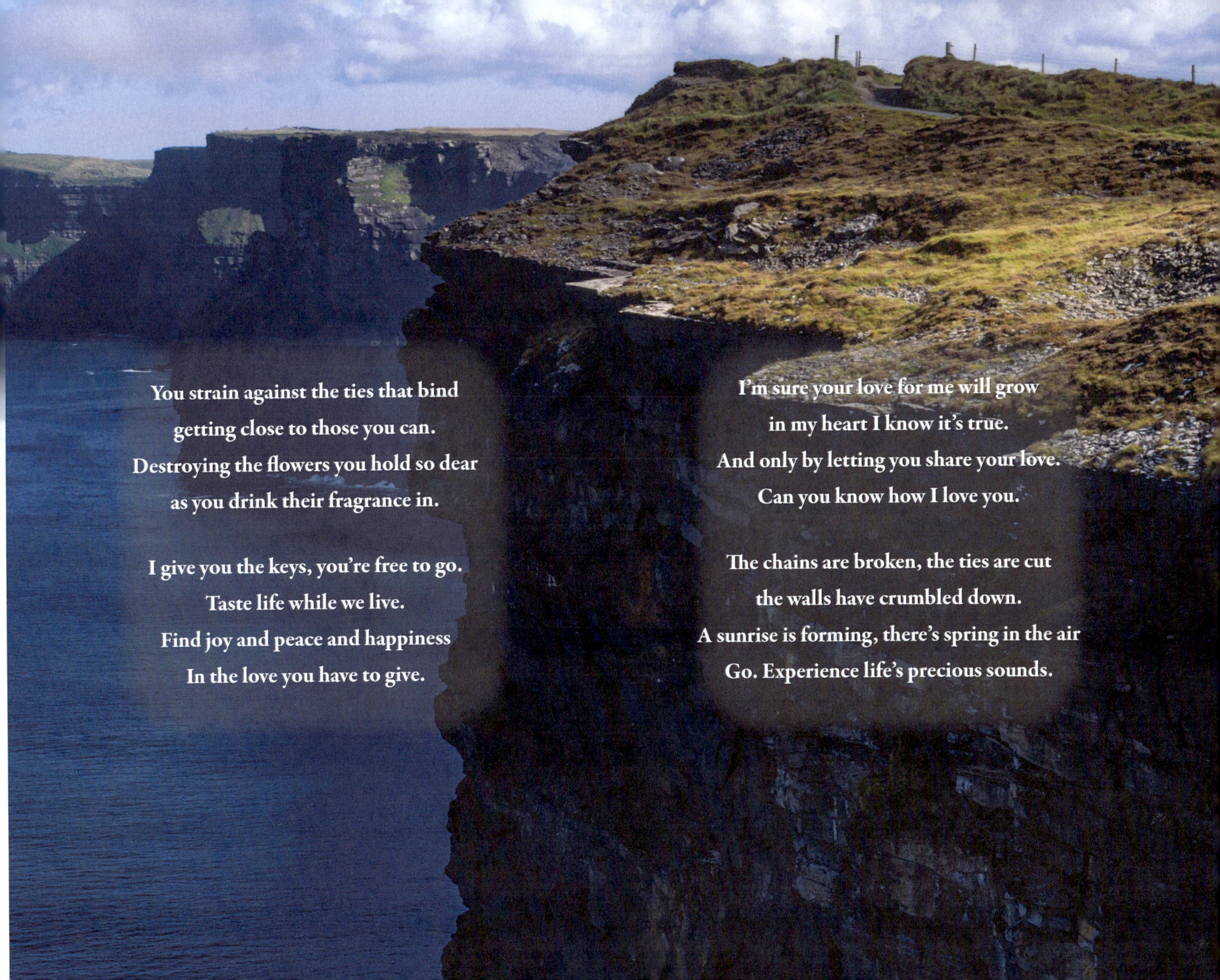

You strain against the ties that bind
getting close to those you can.
Destroying the flowers you hold so dear
as you drink their fragrance in.

I give you the keys, you're free to go.
Taste life while we live.
Find joy and peace and happiness
In the love you have to give.

I'm sure your love for me will grow
in my heart I know it's true.
And only by letting you share your love.
Can you know how I love you.

The chains are broken, the ties are cut
the walls have crumbled down.
A sunrise is forming, there's spring in the air
Go. Experience life's precious sounds.

Pirate's Cave

Deep secluded canyon cove.

Powder white sandy shore.

A small mysterious pirate cave

with watery front door.

Waves come rushing in and out

tempting little thieves,

to try and steal the treasure out

each time the water leaves.

A splash and giggle as one gets caught

now soaked up to the knee

undaunted by the chilling affect

of this small catastrophe.

The cave is empty, the treasure's gone

still, the quest goes on.

For it's not what's there, It's getting there

That makes it all the fun.

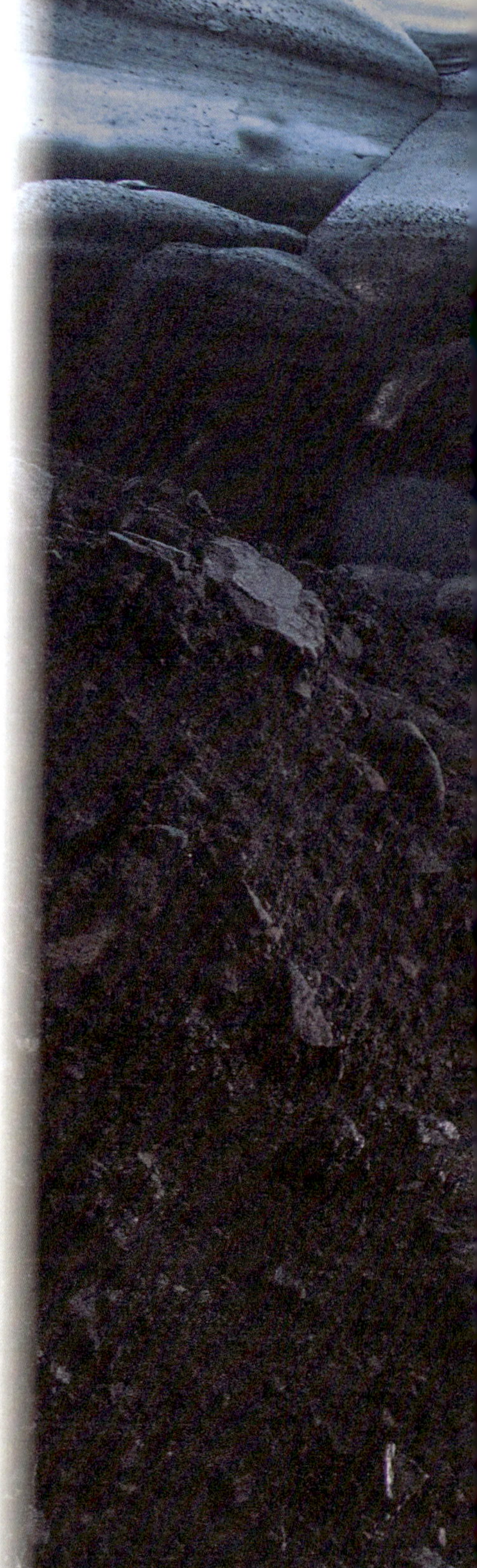

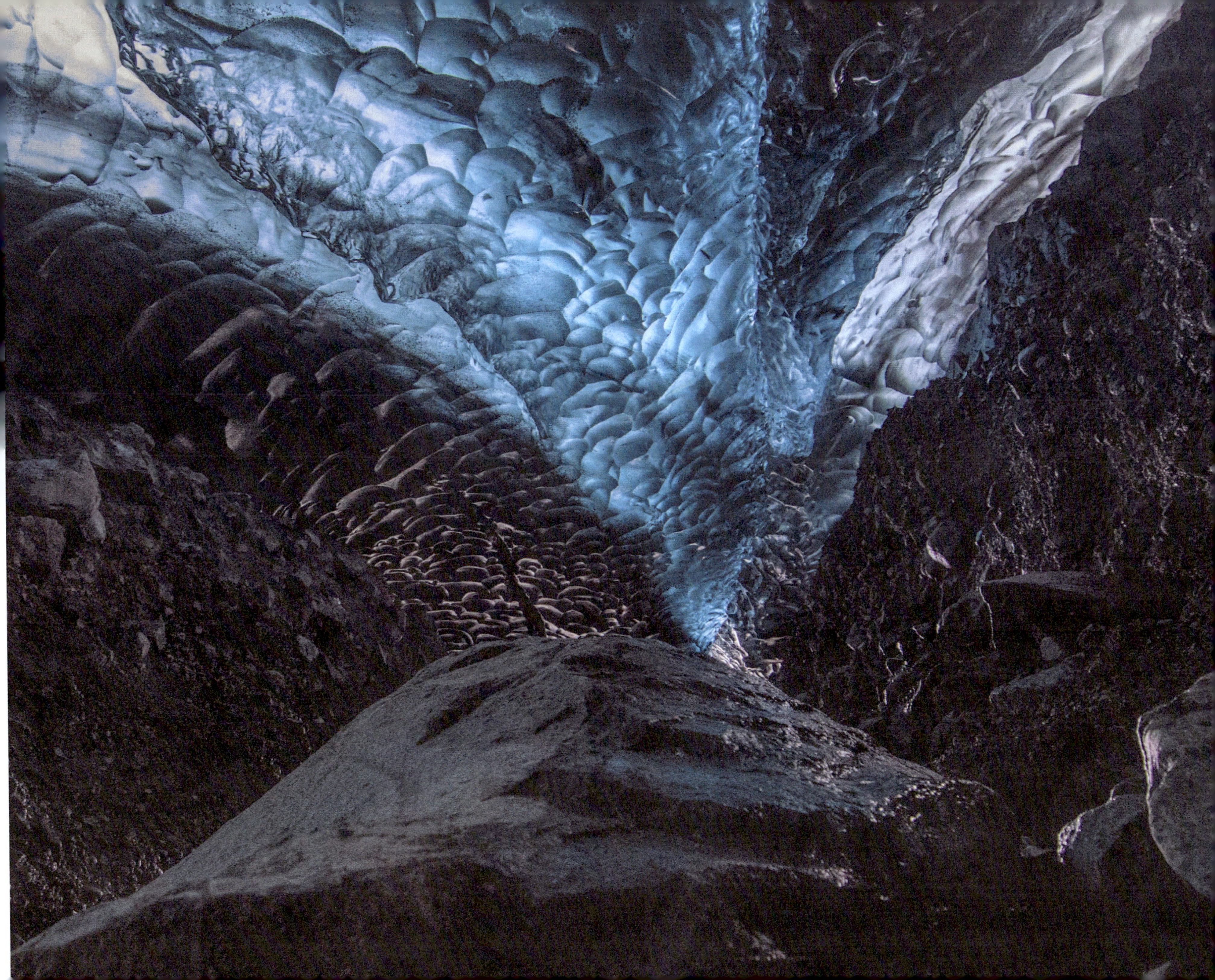

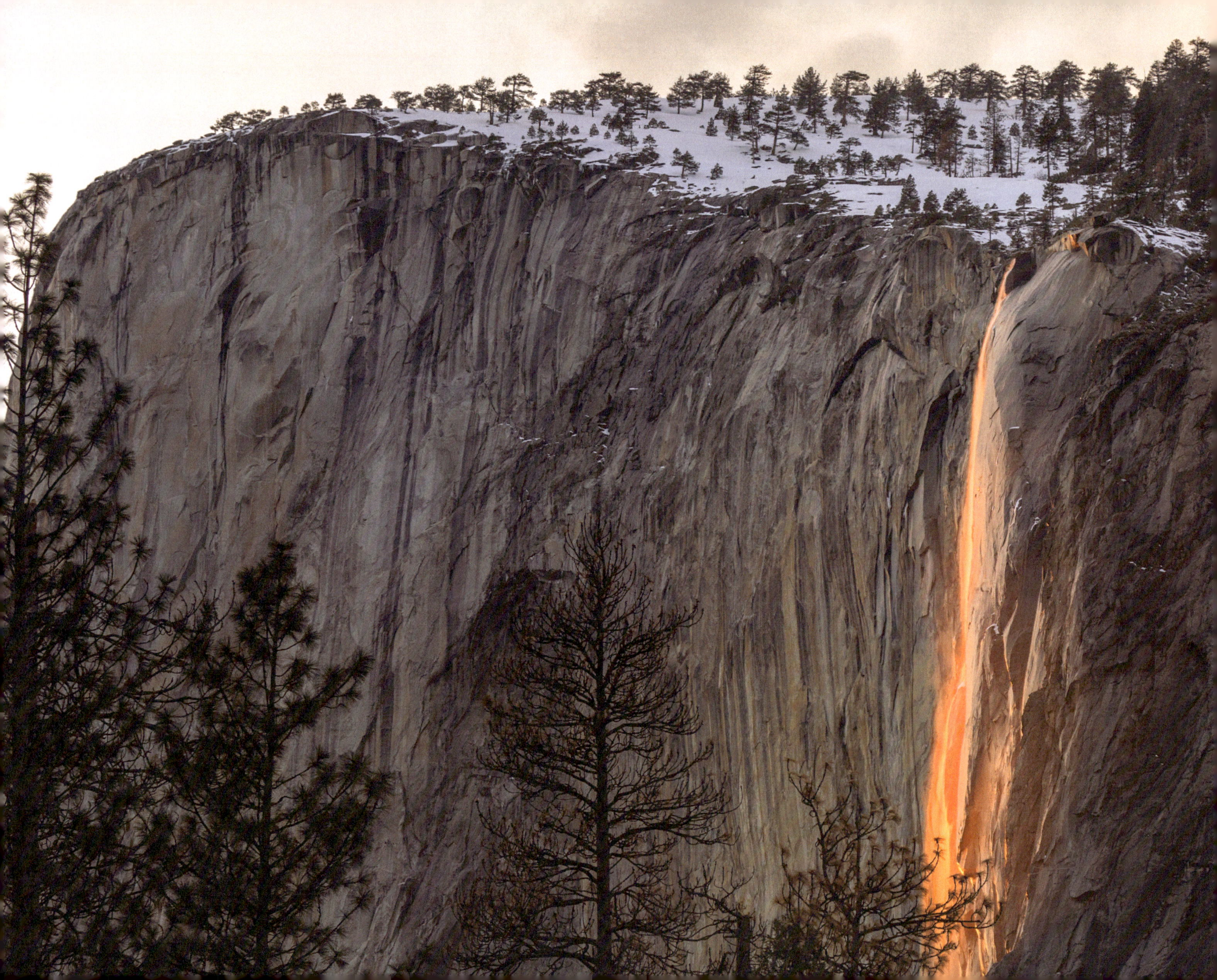

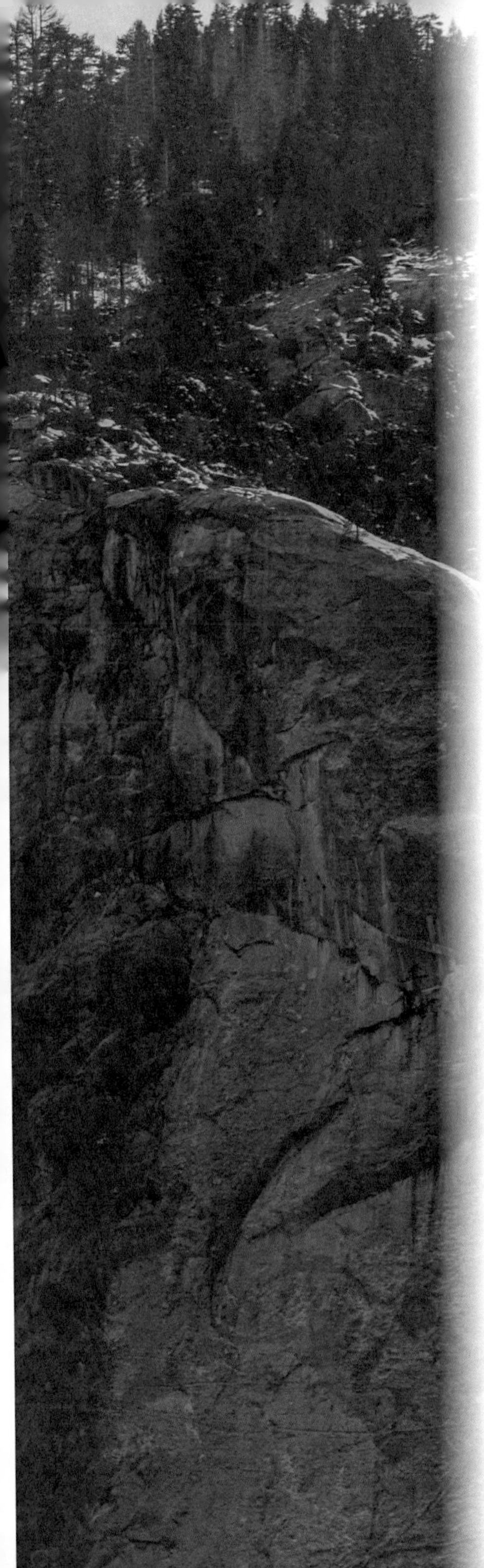

Sing Me Your Song

Though your words may be sharp,
your emotions flat
and your soul sings a mournful song.
I know in you a rhapsody plays,
Which to share your heart once longed.

You've uttered a line
or hummed a verse
whose notes seemed to fall on deaf ears.
So to stop the pain you took it back

which seemed to calm your fears.
I want you to know that I heard it all
each note, each hum, and each verse.
I cherish each one, and I know now,
I couldn't have treated you worse.

Open your soul and sing me your song,
you command my devoted ear.
Play with confidence your song of love.
And I will surely hear.

Zin

The essence extracted
the life ex-pressed
the broken body discarded and left.

All that it was
is now all that it is
the purity and truth and power that gives.

This life blood breathes
Devours and grows.
Its body enhances and flowers the nose.

The will now harnessed
the attitude refined,
sharp memories are faded with the passing of time.

A life condensed
into a single drip.
An entire season revealed in a sip.

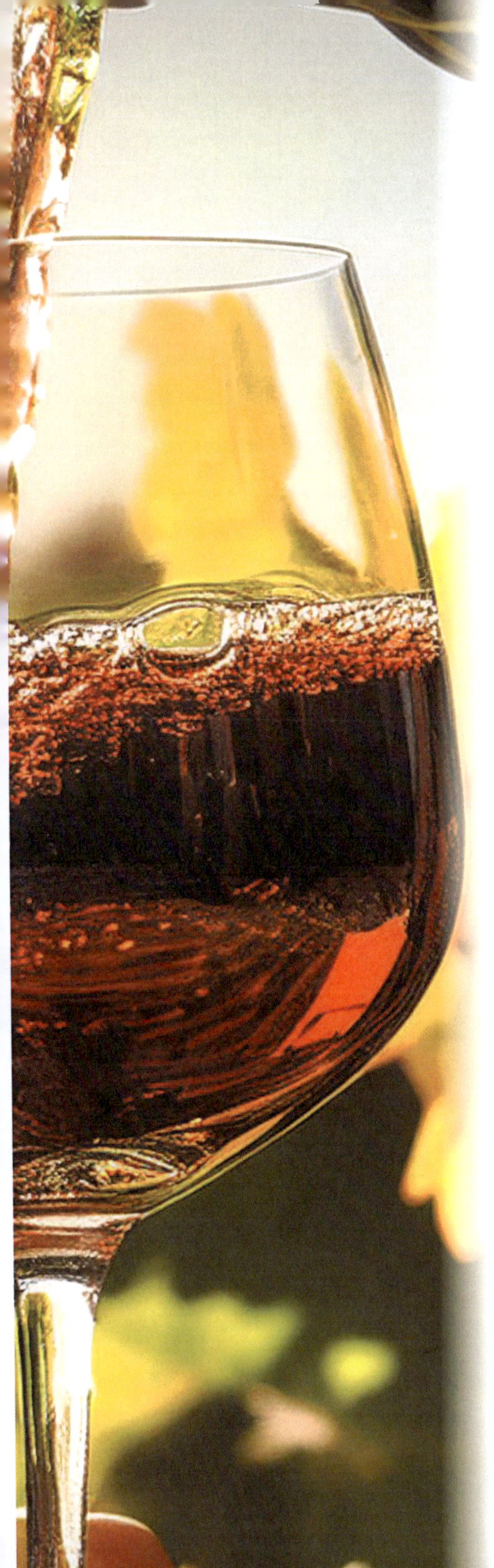

Over the years I have grown to love wine. At one point I made my way through Paso Robles, California and discovered the great many wineries in the region and one of the wine varietals they're known for is Zinfandel. It's a big wine. Bold flavors, deep colors, complex fruit, one of the biggest wines you can think of, and my favorite Zin maker was Tobin James winery. If you make your way through there stop by and try their reserve zin and you'll fall in love just as I have.

My Sun

Sultry seductive sandy shore,
ocean calm and blue.
Slowly sinking over the horizon
painting a rosy hue.

Warm and safe, we watch in awe,
all nature not a sound.
As you gently kiss the world good-night,
and silently lie down.

Slowly, sweetly, no look back,
today your job is through,
tomorrow you'll rise and kiss our cheek
and start our day out new.

You lift our spirits and warm our hearts
our souls belongs to you
for when you're away, the skies turn gray
and paint our spirits blue.

Eternal fire, yellow star,
You mean the world to me.
But the universe is vast,
and I am so small,
what can I possibly mean to thee?

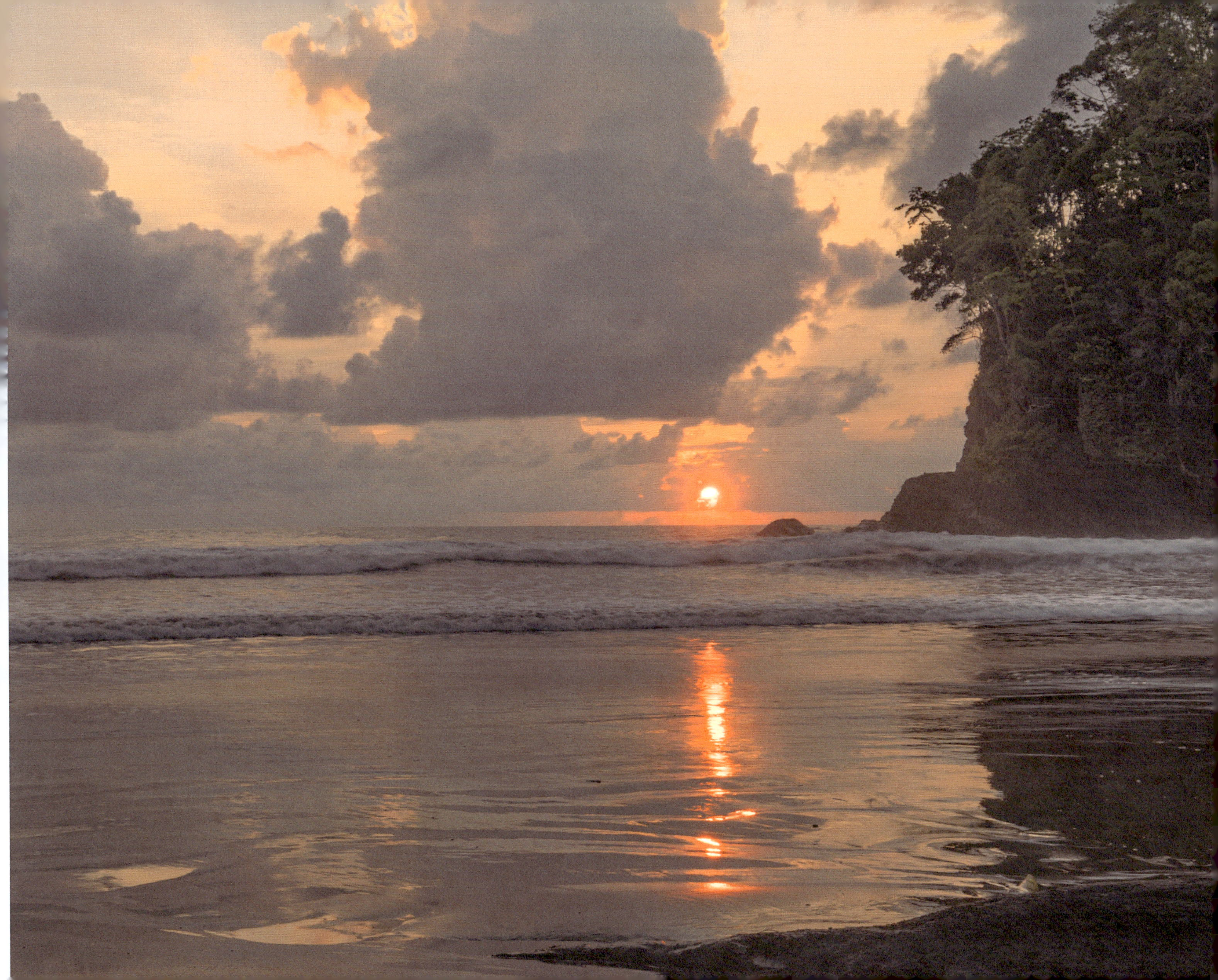

Warm Thoughts of You

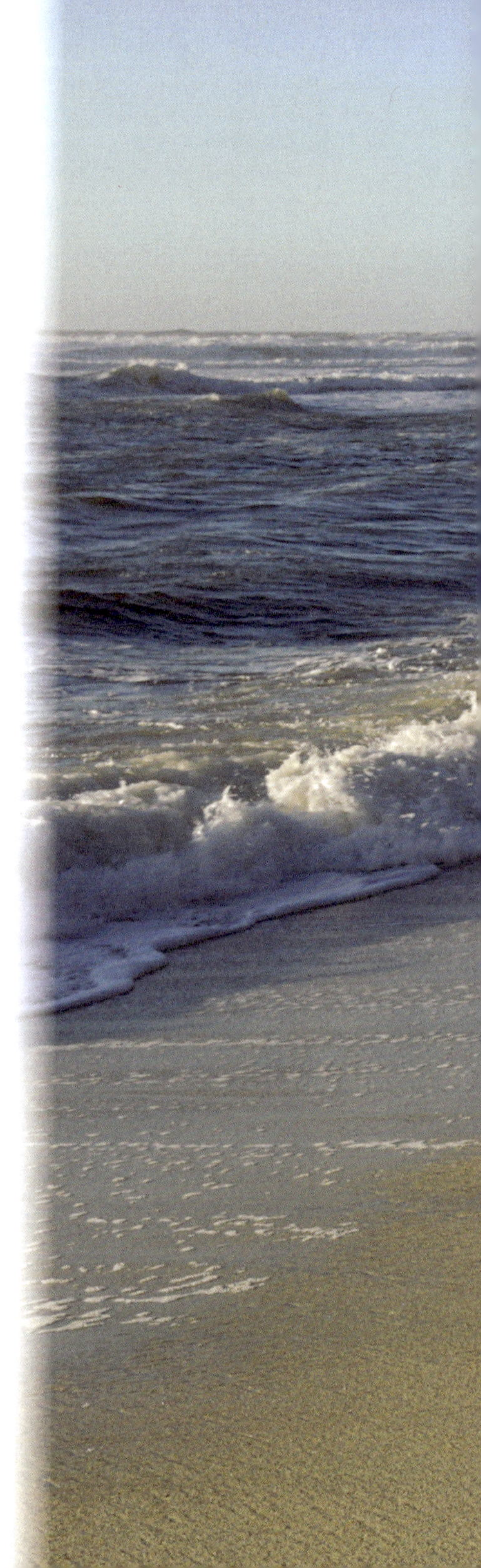

Shadows fall before me
as I walk along the shore.
The ocean cries my name,
but I quietly ignore.

The wind is driving at my back,
the waves grab at my feet.
But my mind is in another place,
another world I see.

The sun's suspended above the horizon,
hanging by a thread.
Soon the string will at last be cut
and sink into a pool of red.

As I await the setting sun
the gulls join in the watch,
lining up along the shore
filling every empty spot.

The wind blows hard and sends a chill,
an attempt to break my trance.
Then waves call to me, but do not succeed
with their seductive dance.

I came to see the setting sun
to that my heart stays true.
I came to see the setting sun
and think warm thoughts of you.

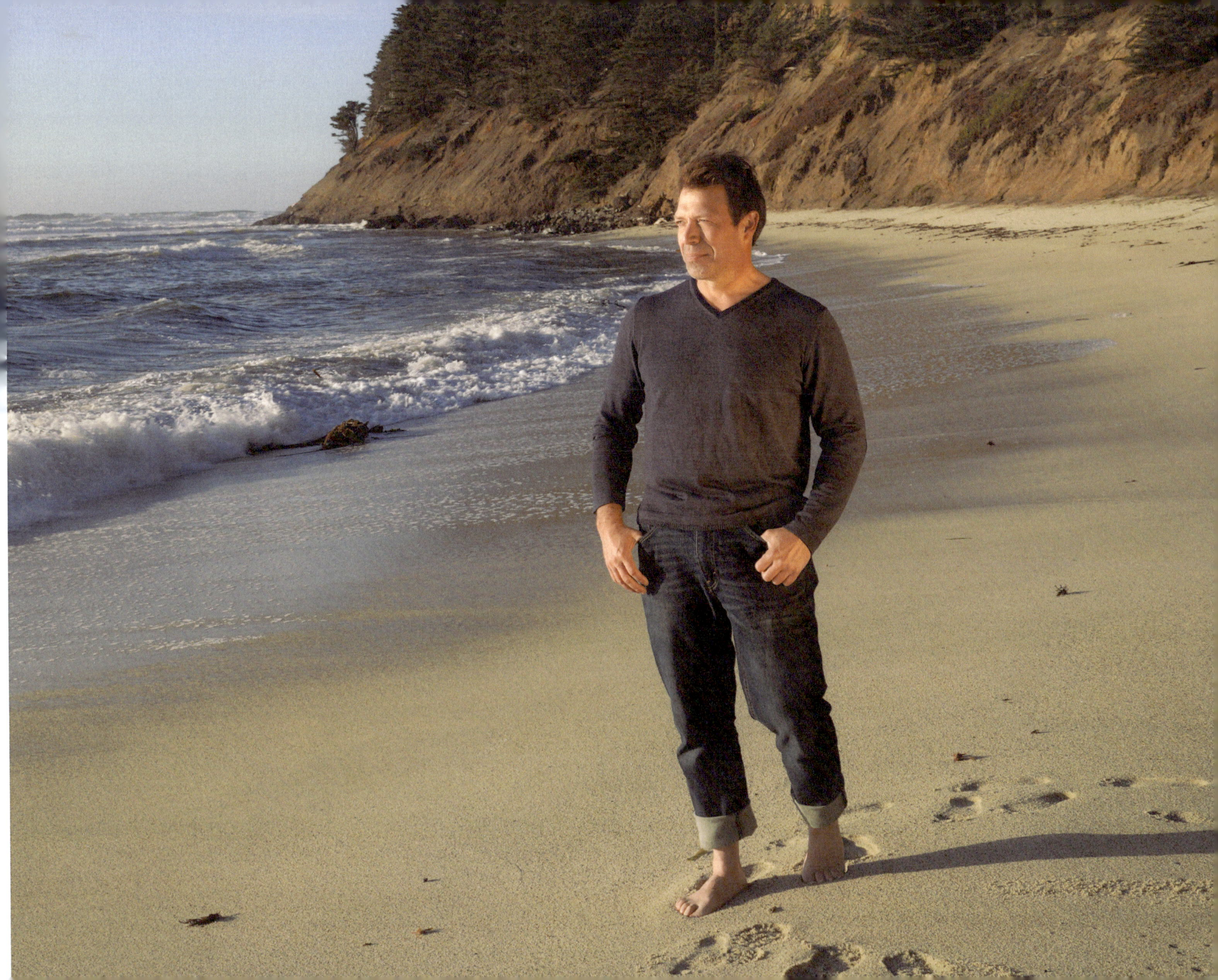

Voices in the Sea

Can you hear it?

Listen!

There!

Can you hear the low rumble of men's voices

as they sit in the living room

talking about the things men talk about?

Can you hear the muffled laughter as they chuckle amongst them-
selves?

And there!

Can your hear the women in the kitchen

their soft voices, barely a whisper.

And the clinking of the dishes as they prepare the meal.

And the children!

Can you hear them?

Can you hear the giggles and laughter

as they chase each other through the house

through the kitchen

through the living room

can you hear the voices?

Shhhhhhhhhh.................

Listen.

Listen to the sea.

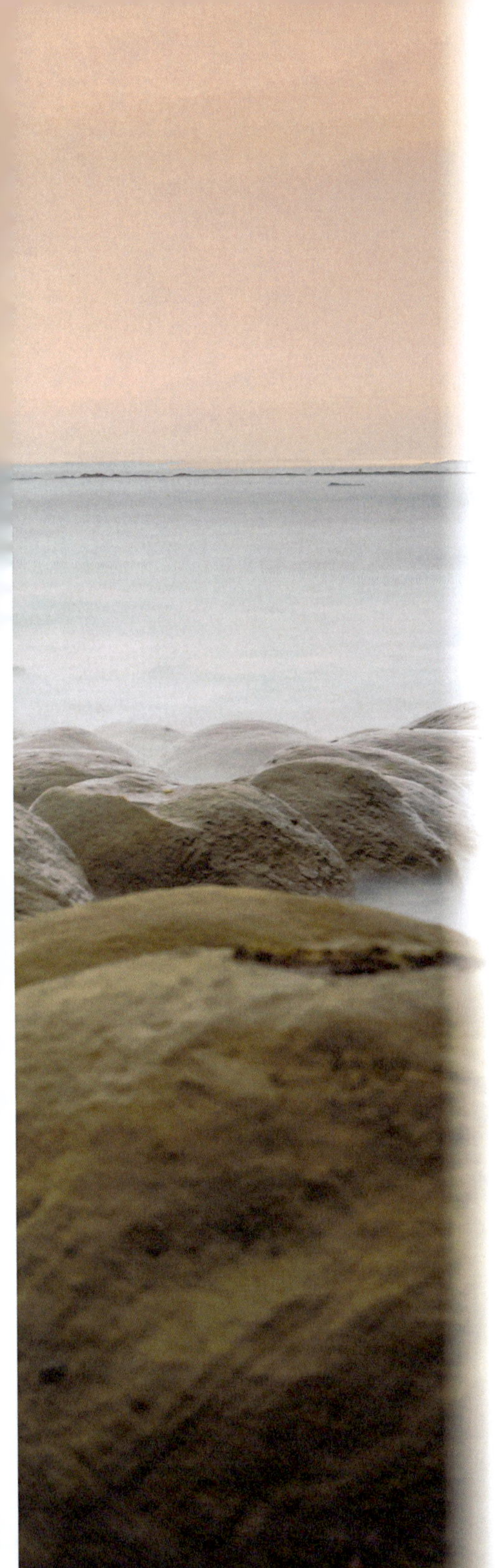

The ocean waves crash against each other, the shore, docks, ships, and themselves. And in that raucous banter what do you hear? Voices from the past calling to us, voices from the future warning us? Songs of life as old as the world? Echoes carried on the wind from a time long ago? Is it the same song that has been repeated for millions of years or is this a new composition never before heard? What do you hear?

The Tide is Out

The tide is out
and the beach is ours.

We walk along leaving our tracks,
building our sand castles,
and soaking up the sun.

We are content.
We are ignorant.
We are absorbed in our own cares and pleasures.

We run along the beach
kicking sand into the wind
and flirting with the ocean
as it waits impatiently.

But soon,
soon the sun will go down
and the ocean will rise up

to erase what is left of you and me.

And the beach will be pure and clean once again.

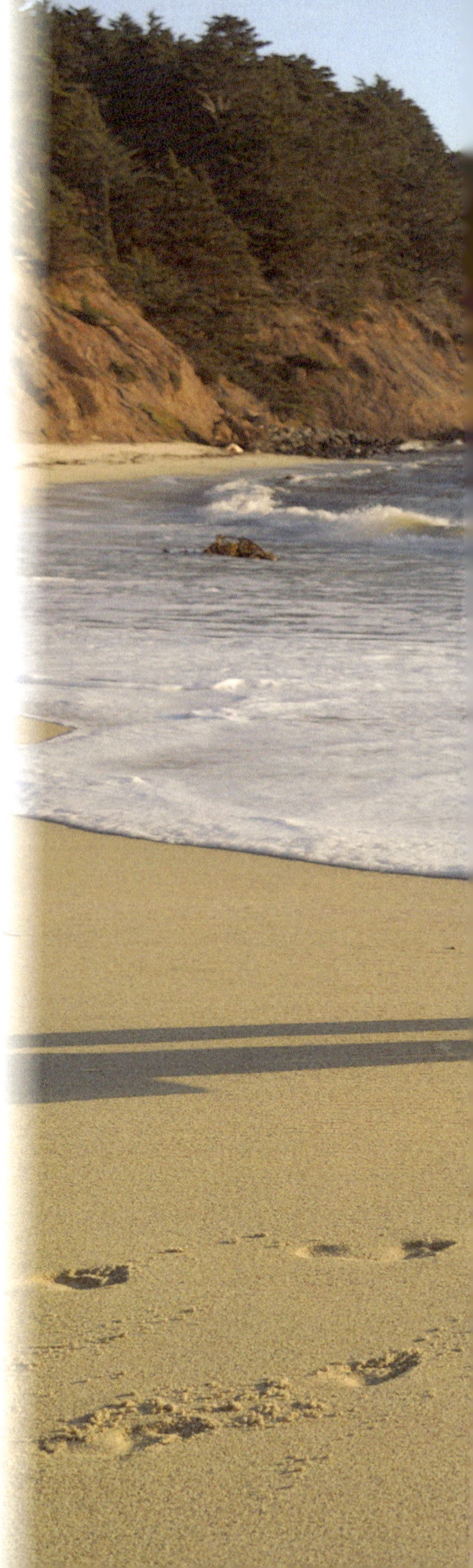

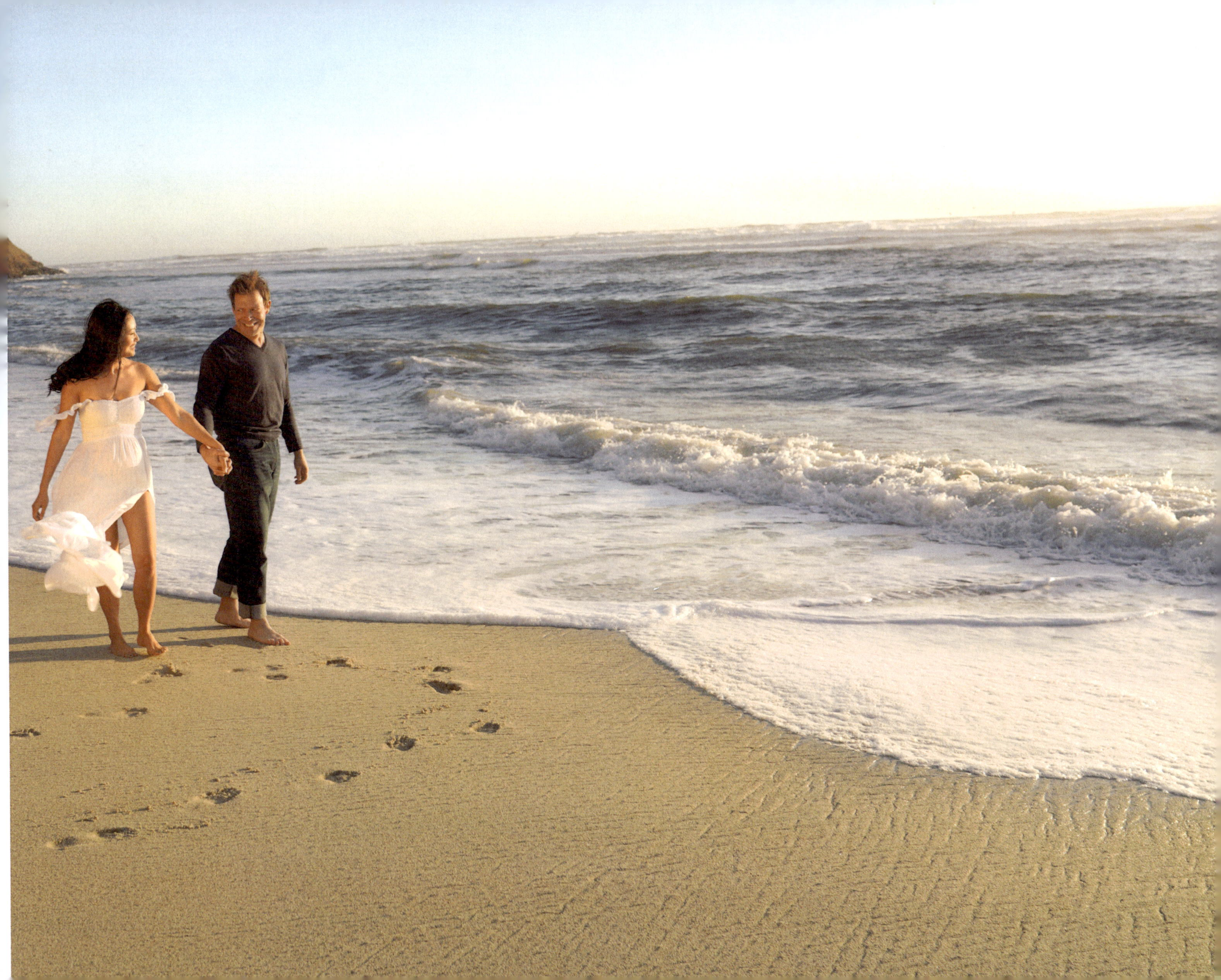

Turn the Page

Ink blood
Paper Life
Pain release
Skeleton confront
Past disclose
Future expose
Spirit reborn
Life renew
Sorrow end
Healing begin
Say it.
Write it.
Paint it.
Express it.
Then turn the page.

Art is a powerful thing not only to the one observing, but also to the one creating. The passion, emotion, pain, love, desire, lust, compassion, sorrow, the heart poured onto the page through paint, ink, pencil, words, and pictures is an attempt to purge this torment from our soul. The conflict within and our desire to make sense of it drives us to express it. Once out we can look at it, still feel it, but then turn the page and continue on.

I Will Sleep

The ocean whispers my name.

The moon guides my soul.

The wind blows but I feel not.

The waves crash but I am unmoved.

My eyes are gray.

My heart has drowned in sorrow.

My spirit has seeped out amongst my tears.

I am but an empty shell.

Walk out deep.

Don't look back.

Let the roar of the waves consume me

And float away.

Darkness will come.

The calm, quiet darkness,

And I will sleep.

Yes,

Forever will I sleep.

Bipolar disorder runs in my family. It used to be called Manic-Depressive which I believe is much more descriptive. When I am in love nothing can hold me down. When love leaves I am as low as the grave. I have often rationalized saying that without pain how can we know what joy is? Without the loss of love how can we feel the tremendous joy there is in loving someone? How can we love a rose without despising the weed? How can we appreciate beauty without acknowledging ugliness? If everything is beautiful then nothing is. Ups and downs are a natural occurrence and to truly enjoy life you must appreciate that sorrow is the only thing that makes the joy possible. Yet, when the pain comes it still hurts.

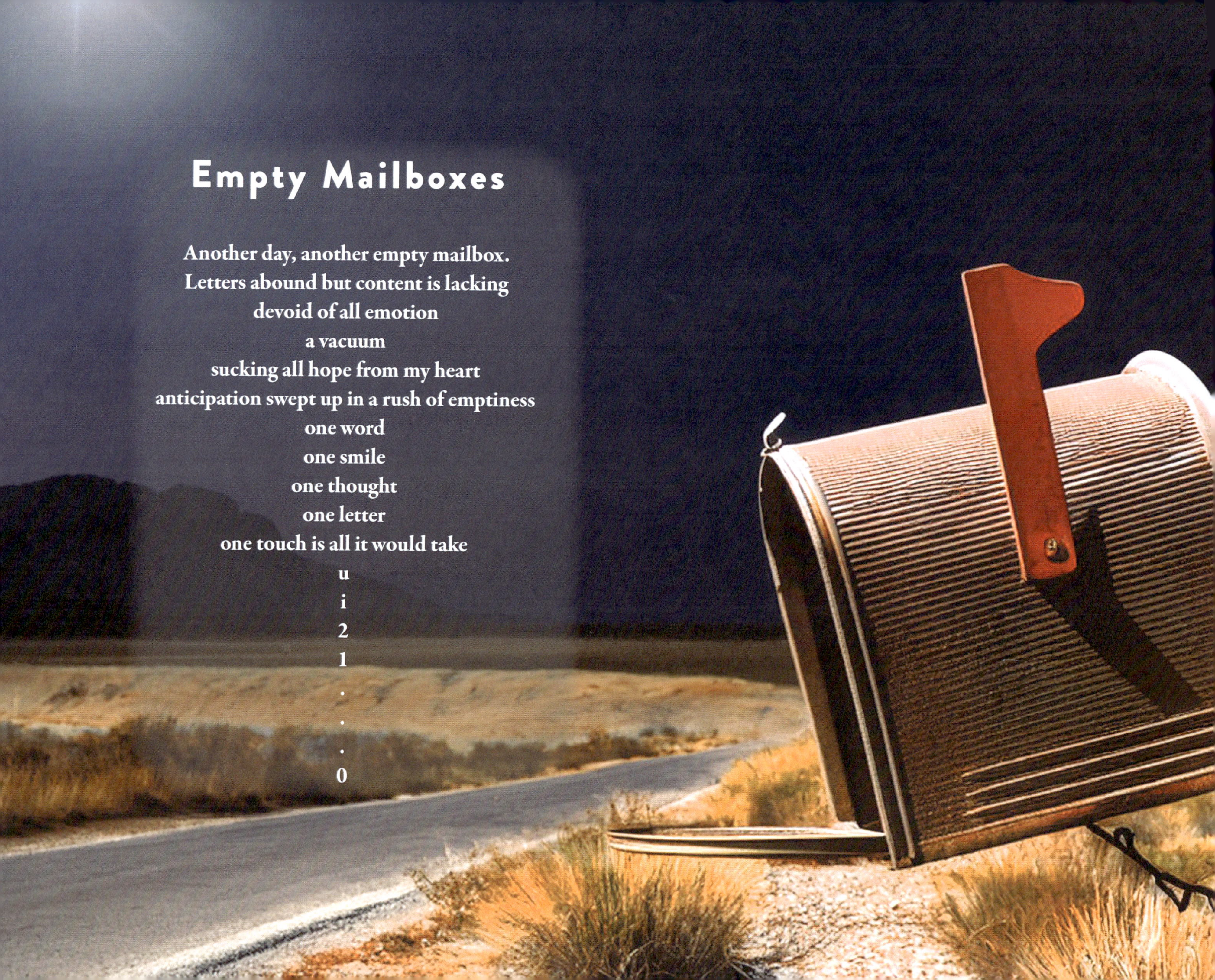

Empty Mailboxes

Another day, another empty mailbox.
Letters abound but content is lacking
devoid of all emotion
a vacuum
sucking all hope from my heart
anticipation swept up in a rush of emptiness
one word
one smile
one thought
one letter
one touch is all it would take
u
i
2
1
.
.
.
.
0

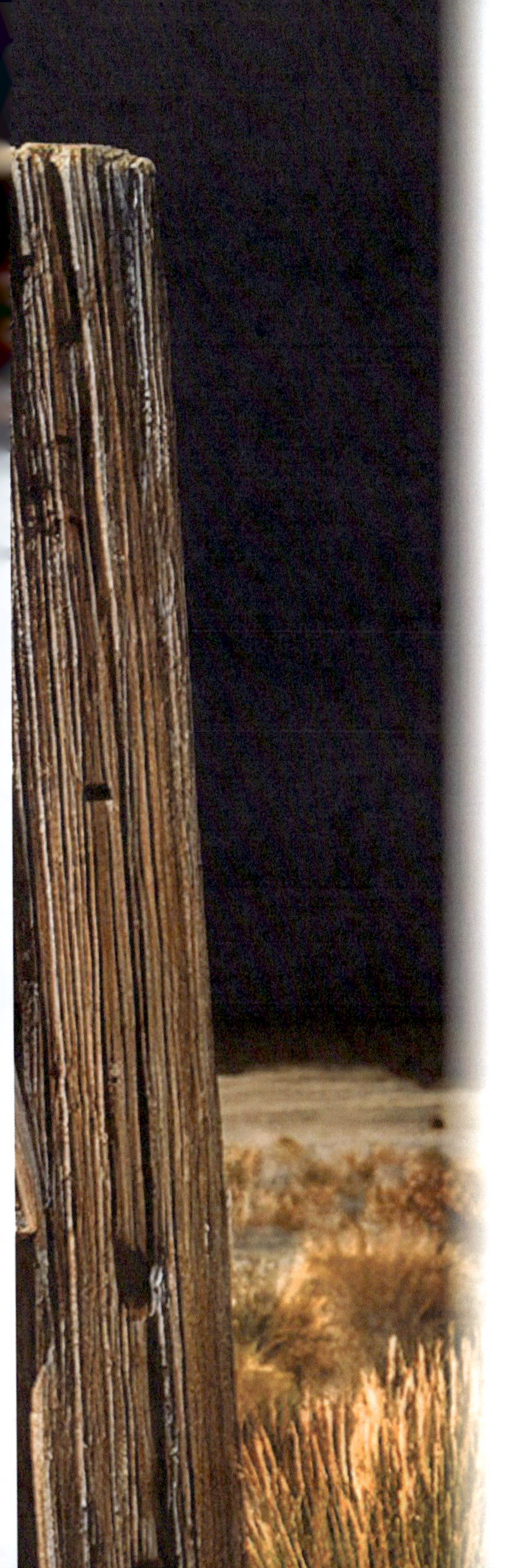

Anticipation. How many times have we gone out to the mailbox excited at what might be there? I am excited every day. So many possibilities await. Is there a package? From whom? What's in it? A letter? From my mom, sister, brother, son, daughter? Now we have internet with instant messages, snap chat, alerts, Twitter, Facebook, Messenger, and on and on. As soon as our phone buzzes or chimes our body reacts. Our heart skips a beat. Our pulse quickens, our hand immediately reaches to pick up the phone. Our eyes search the screen. Who is it, is it her/him? And when it's just junk mail our hearts sink. All that anticipation and hope dashed.

My Muse

Oh, that I could find the words to melt your heart and win your love for me.
For you are my muse, my inspiration, my love unobtainable.
Your beauty captivates me and your music binds me in a spell unbreakable by mortal men.

My heart races at the very thought of you.
My hands tremble at the sound of your voice.
My eyes weep with joy upon seeing your face.

And yet I know that I am unworthy.
A man such as I, whose heart is so fickle.
I shall run a dagger through my own heart before I allow myself to bring harm to yours.
For I know my heart and the hearts of men like me.
To us love is just a dream, a vision unrealized, a mystery whose truth be her very death.
Love is not to be had, but to be dreamt.
For the very touch of it causes it to whither away.
What once dazzled the stars and made the roses blush,
Now holds no more worth than a tarnished penny.
As Midas once had the golden touch, we hold the touch of doom.

So love, my love, for me is you.
My life, my inspiration, the reason for the very beating of my heart.
For you my heart sings, the words flow, my pen skates across page after page.
My mind whirls and my fingers stumble trying to keep pace.
I feel my heart beating in my throat, temples throbbing,
Such excitement grips me and forces my hand to write.

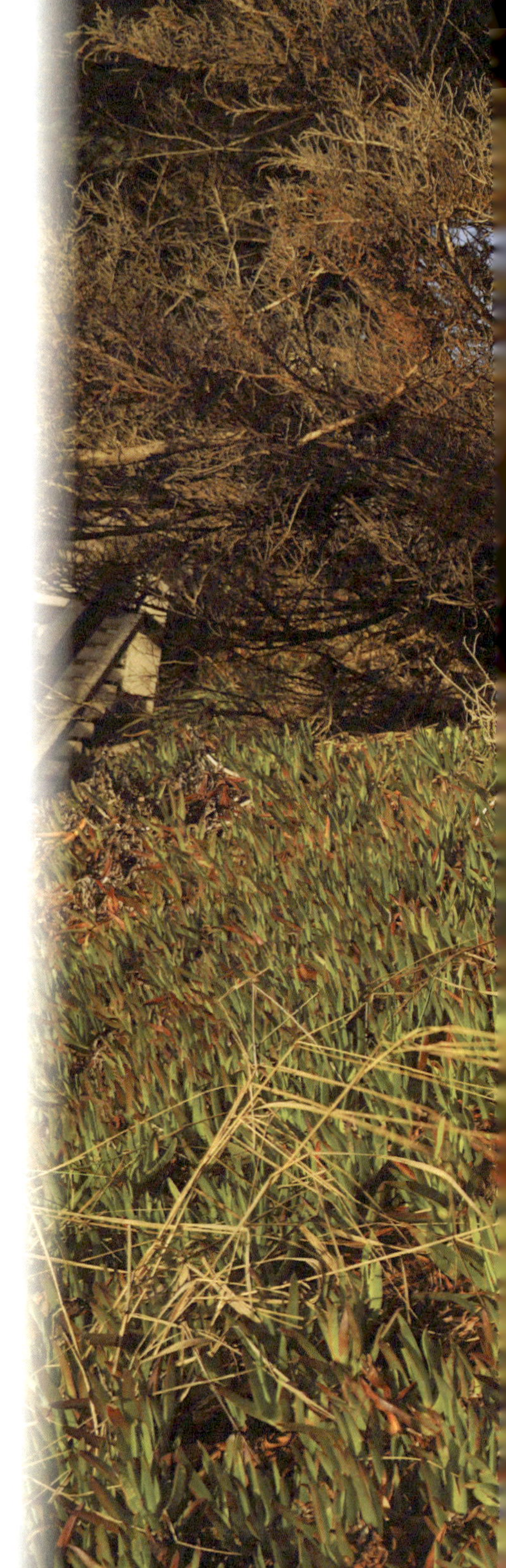

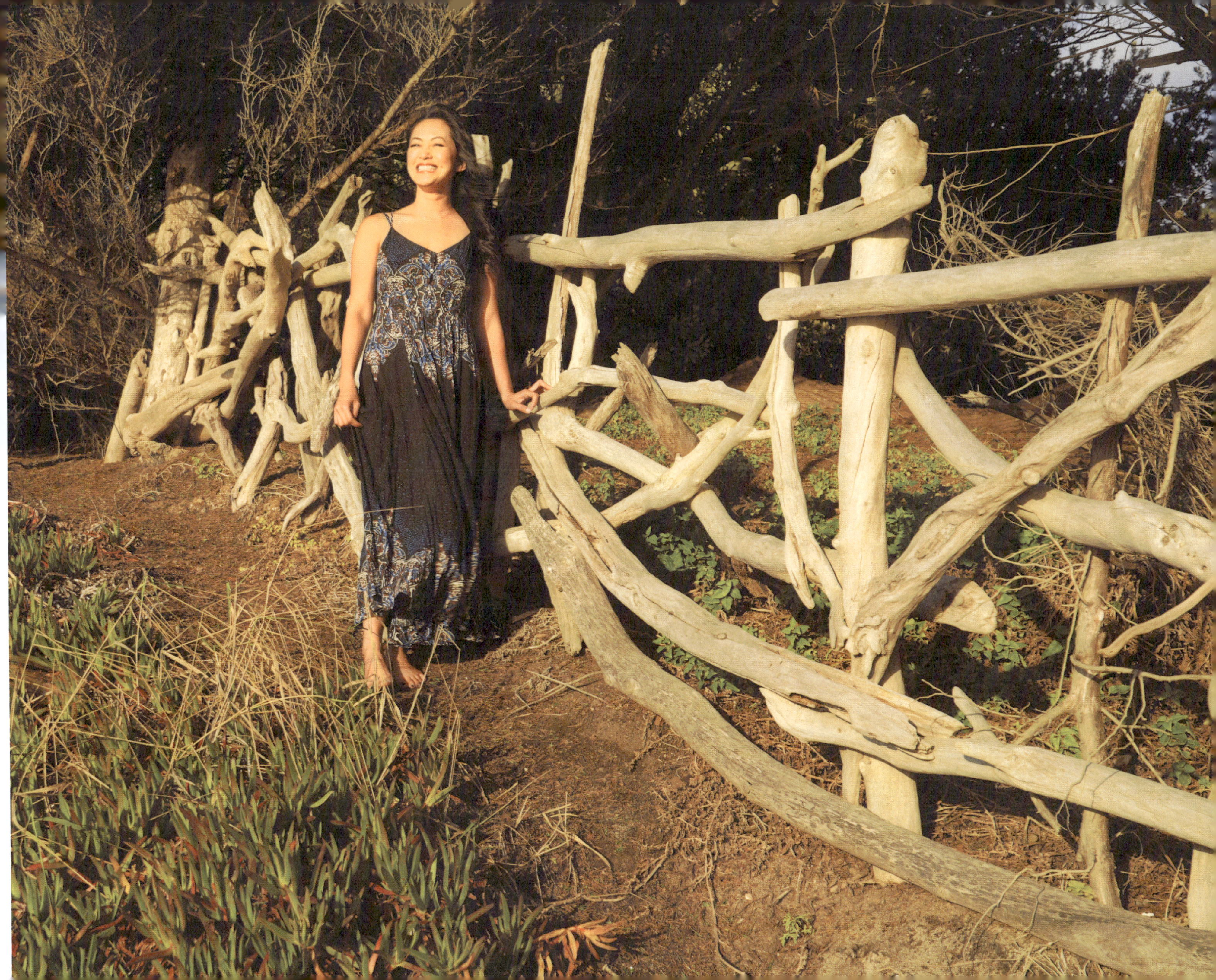

So tonight my words go out to you.
From my pen, to the paper, to your heart.
I can picture your eyes as you read, your face,
Your lips moving ever so slightly yet silently.

Your mind racing trying to grasp the depth of my meaning,
then you see.
Your memory is my muse.
You need do nothing, and best yet that you do nothing at all.
For if your heart were ever to admit love for mine,
My heart would surely become blind to the love it once saw.
As once I wrote, "lost love lasts," what never was, could never end.
To admit it would be death.

My heart writes best when it is in love.
And always I find my love is for the dream and not the reality.
So much passion and intensity could never be,
for when acted out the players stumble.
The first take is never perfect and by the time it is perfected,
the scene is old, the lines practiced, the passion now but an act.
Love is a play enjoyed only by the writer and the audience,
The actors but go through the motions.

So I ask you my love, my muse, my friend
Let me use your memory as my inspiration
And for that I will make you immortal

With every word I write
and every song I sing.

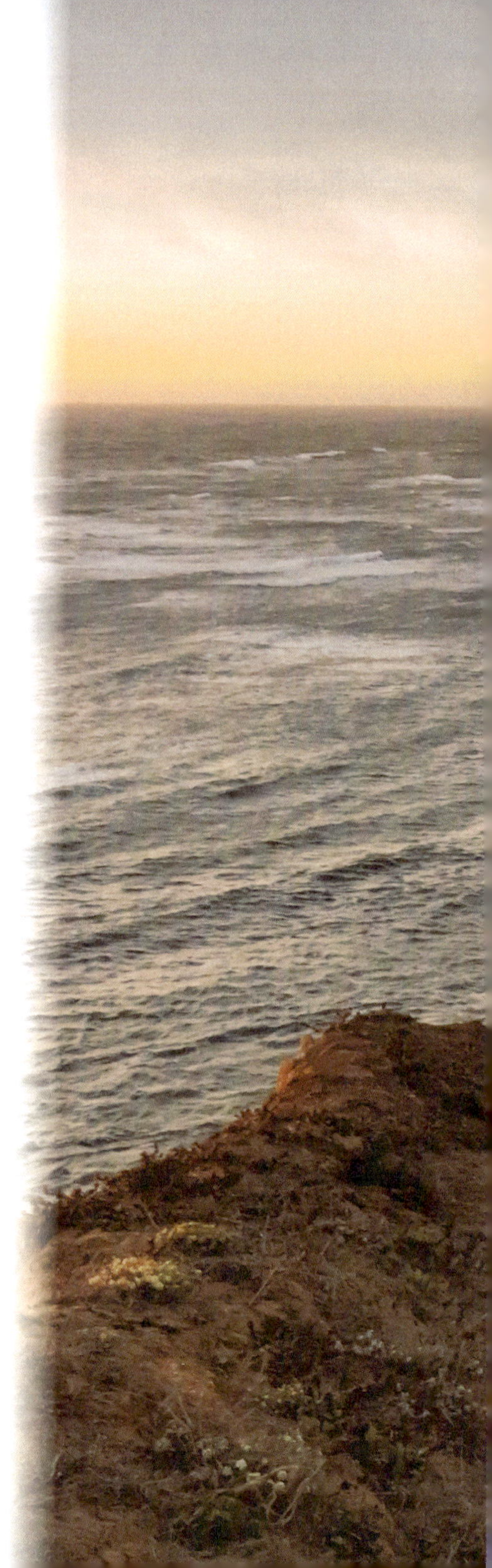

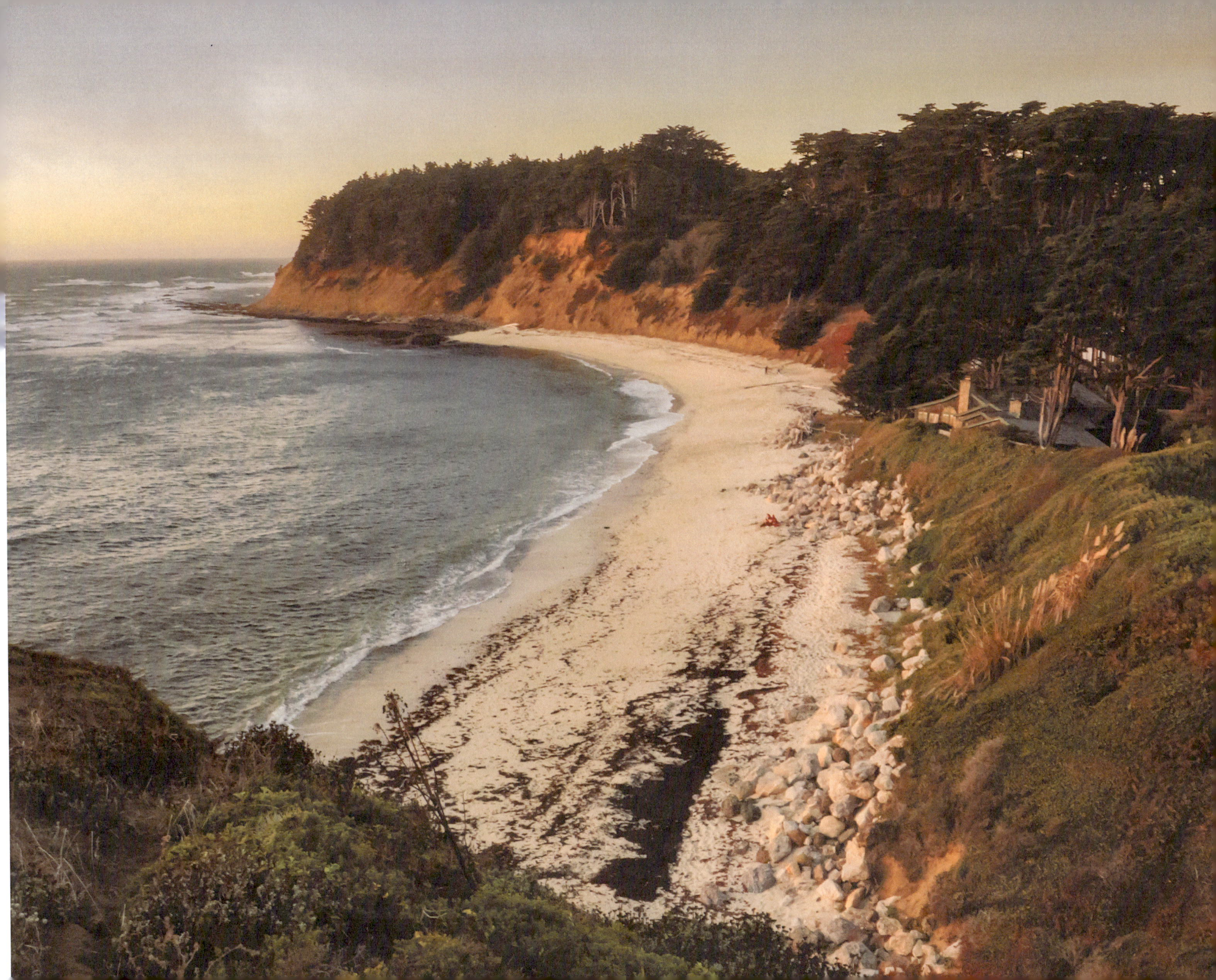

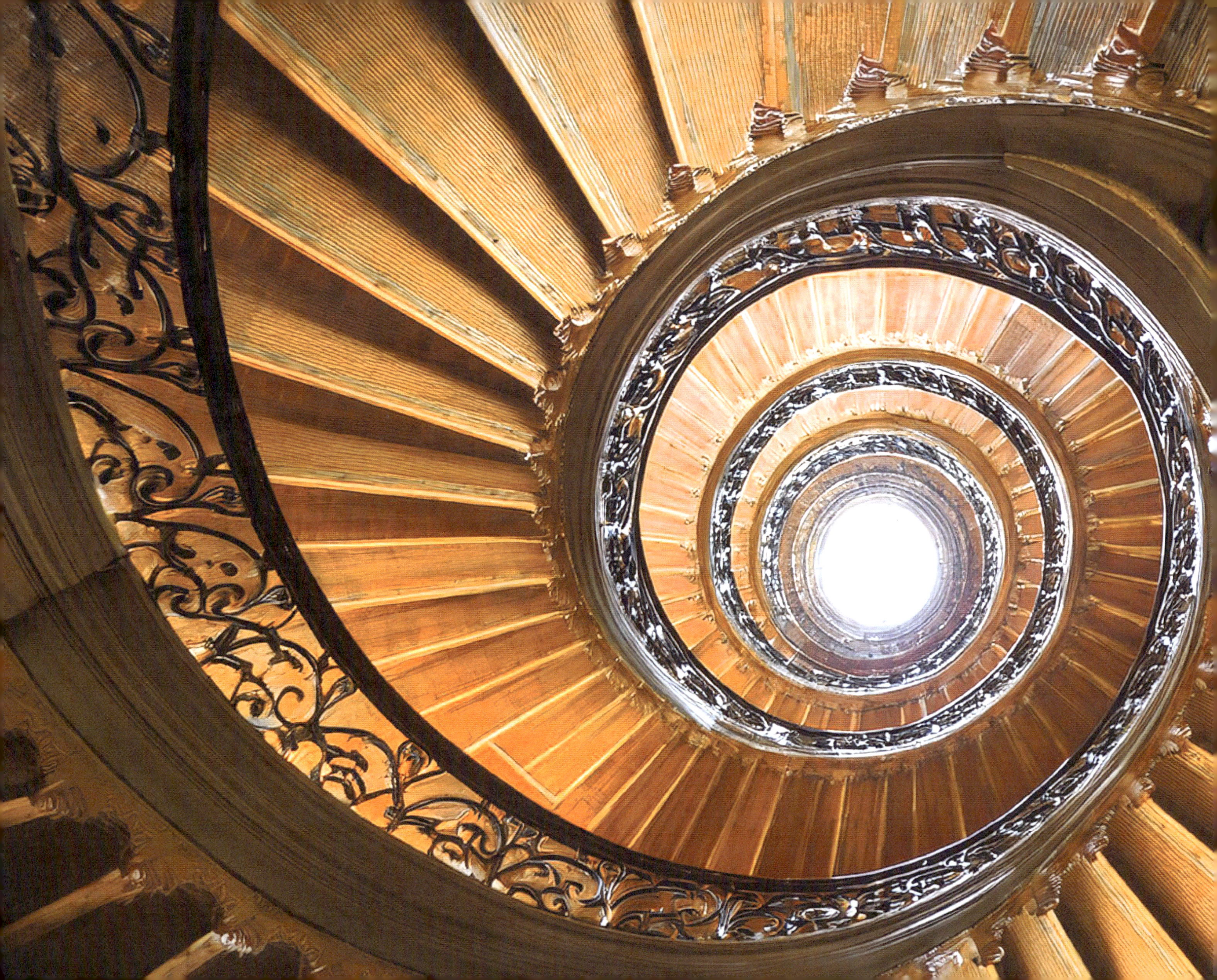

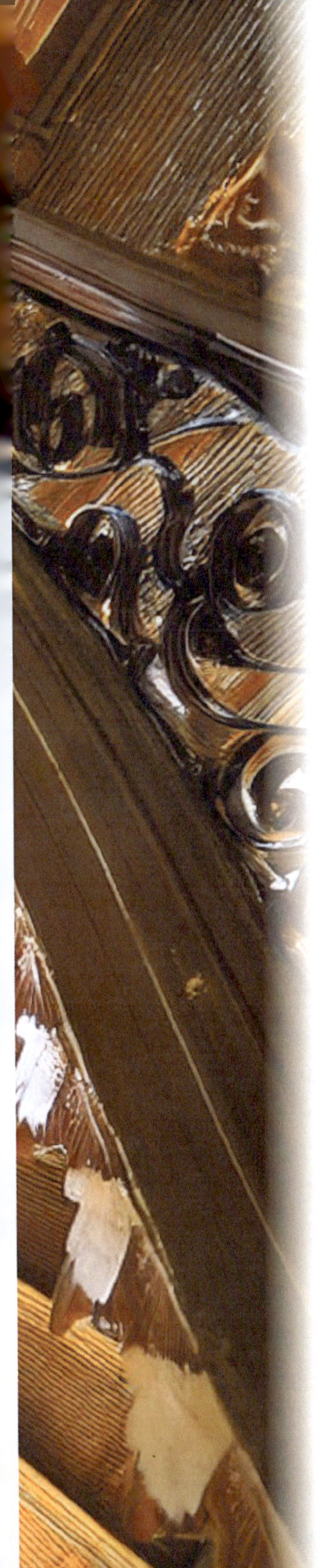

Spirals

'Round and 'round
Always ending where I began
But not quite.

'Round and 'round
Life beginning where it ends
A new light

'Round and 'round
Thoughts spinning in your mind
But out of site.

'Round and 'round
Emotions running 'round your heart
Which one's right?

'Round and 'round
Spirals spinning without end
That's my life.

Suicidal Christmas

'Tis the night before Christmas and all through this house,

Not an emotion is stirring, not inside or out.

Depression engulfs me in waves like the sea,

As alone on the holidays again I will be.

One stocking is hung by the chimney but who cares?

No one will fill it and so it goes bare.

Colorful lights blink yellow, red, blue.

Reminders of Christmases I once shared with you.

But tonight I'm alone in my cold empty bed,

With visions of you with someone else in my head.

My heart is empty and my eyes are full,

Tears brimming inside, my soul lifeless and dull.

I pray to a god I'd long since forgot,

"Please take me tonight for my life is worth not!

Please end this torment and thoughts of regret!

Please take this pain--Have I not suffered enough yet?!"

But the holidays will pass and I'll somehow get by,

'till the next year rolls 'round when I'll wish I could die.

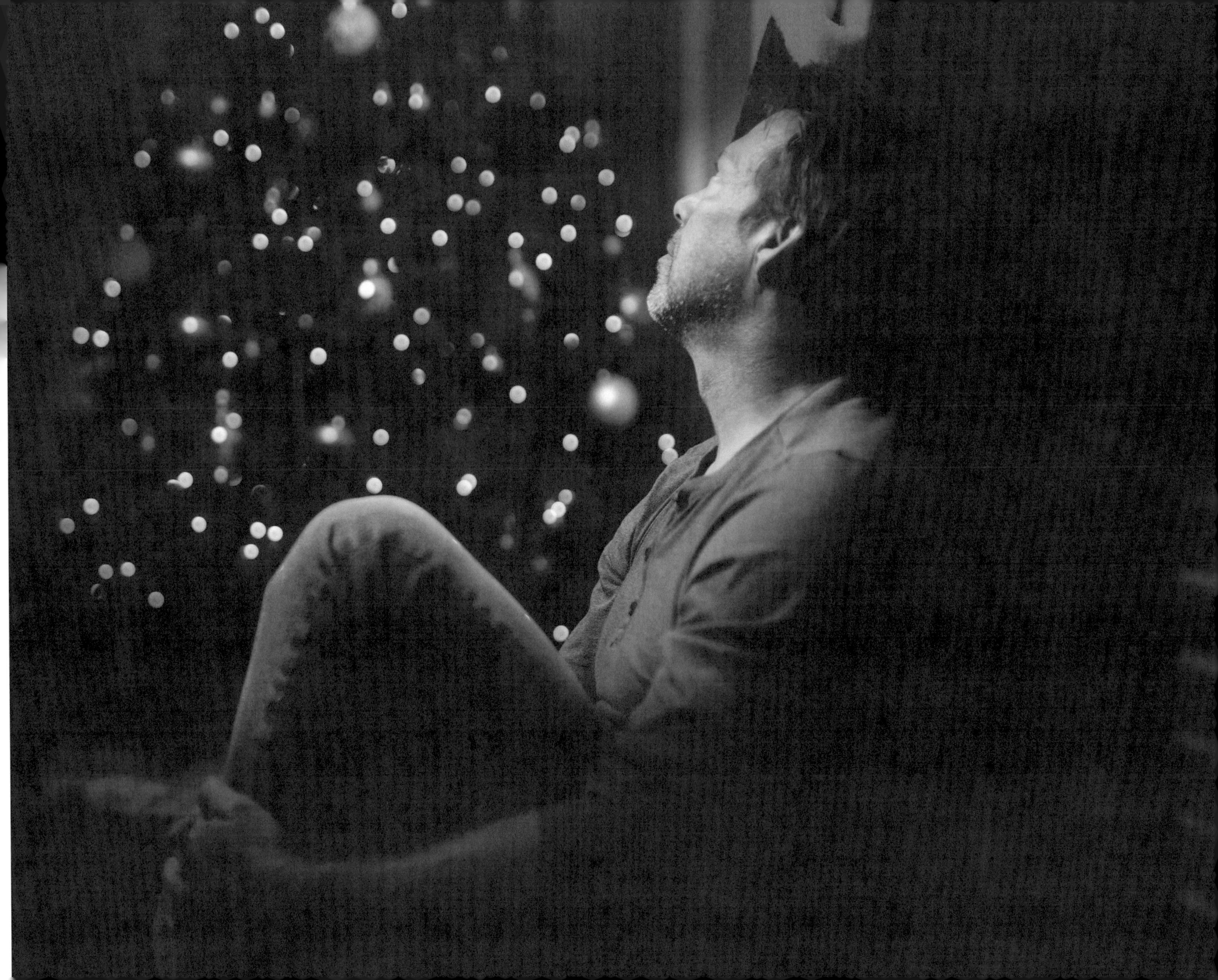

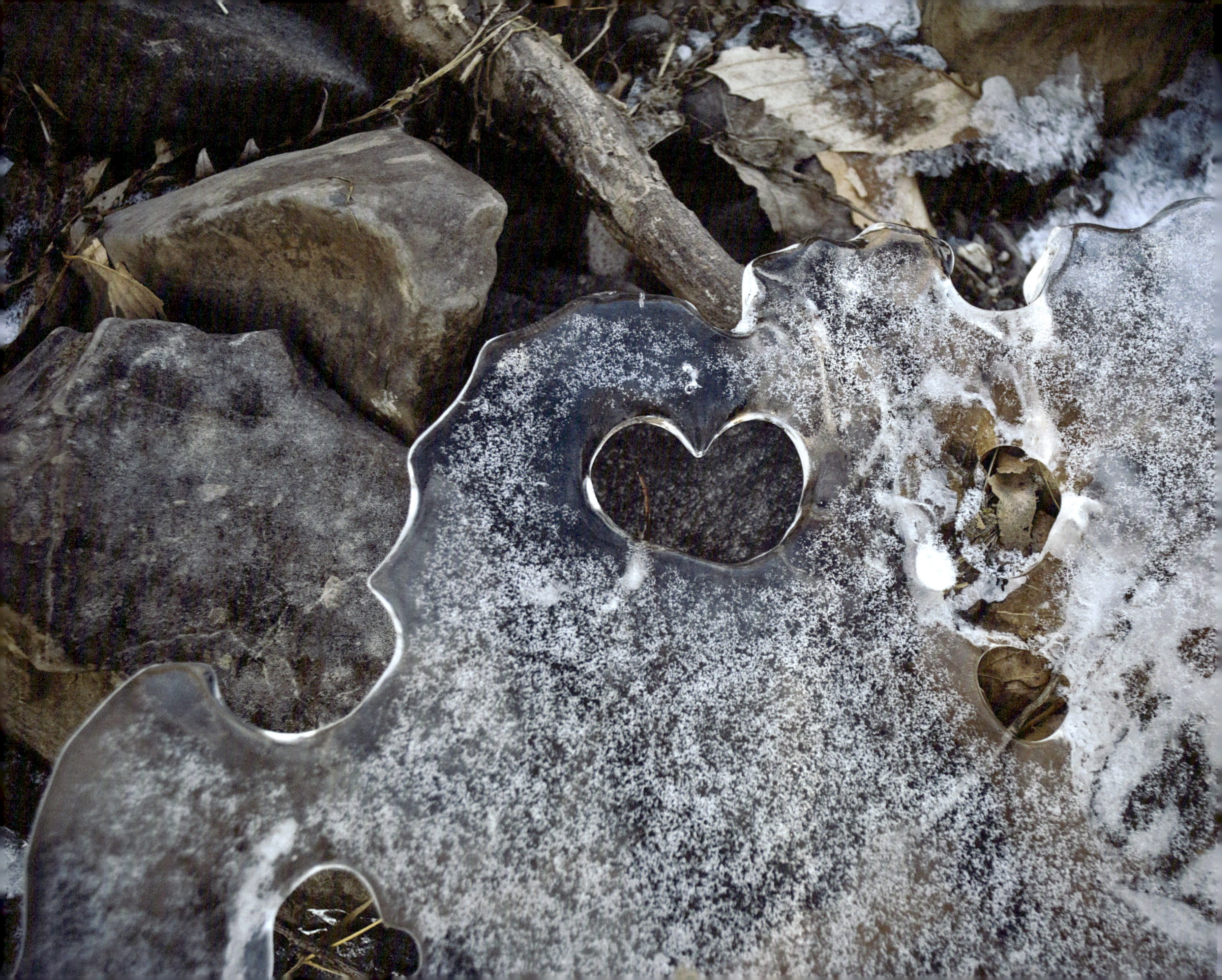

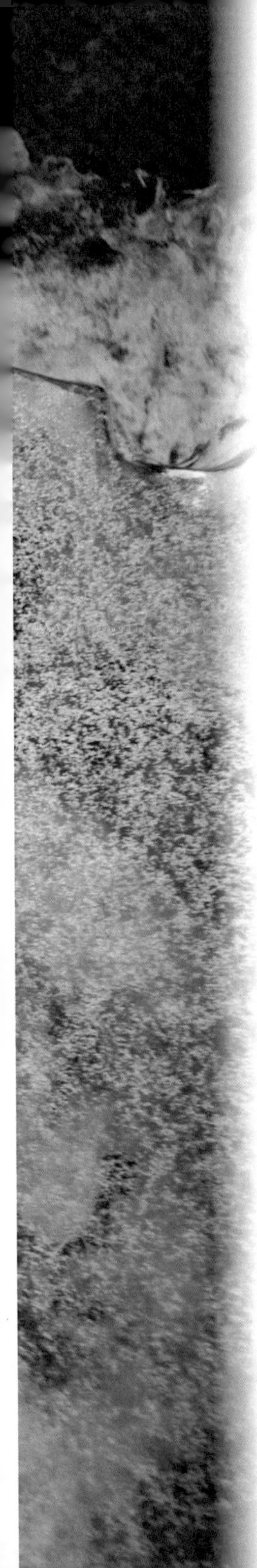

Cupid's Arrow

Stars and moons
both day and night.
Warmth from cold
no wrong, just right.

Soft lips, soft eyes
burn passion inside.
My heart is true
what a shame to hide.

Eyes to eyes and life to life
souls entwine as hearts unite.
Tender the words afraid to say

The heart beats yes but the lips abstain.

Some days, some day the dreams we dream
seem almost real yet only seem.
Our lives slip by one day at a time
as we act out the part of love in mime.

Faces paint dramatic scenes
as words unheard miss eyes unseen.
How cruel the torture,
how real the pain
when Cupid's arrow takes flight without aim.

Waiting on love

You had never asked me
to love you like I do,
so I can only blame myself
for the pain my heart goes through.

My days are never ending fits
of love's dark despair.
My heart swells in anticipation
then sinks 'cause you're not there.

I want to hold you close to me
and whisper in your ear.
I want to brighten up your nights
and take away your fears.

I know we're meant to be together,
I knew it from the start.
But waiting here for you to decide
was too much for my heart.

Yet, now again I wait for you
as torment churns me through.
Waiting for you to realize
how much you love me too.

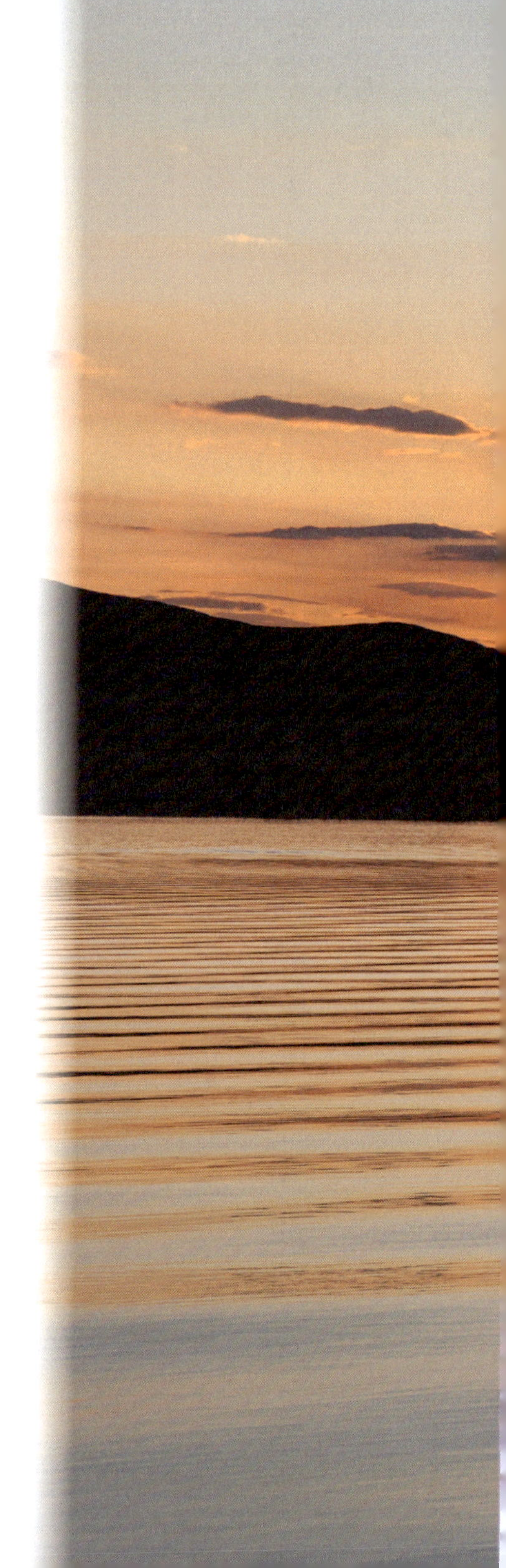

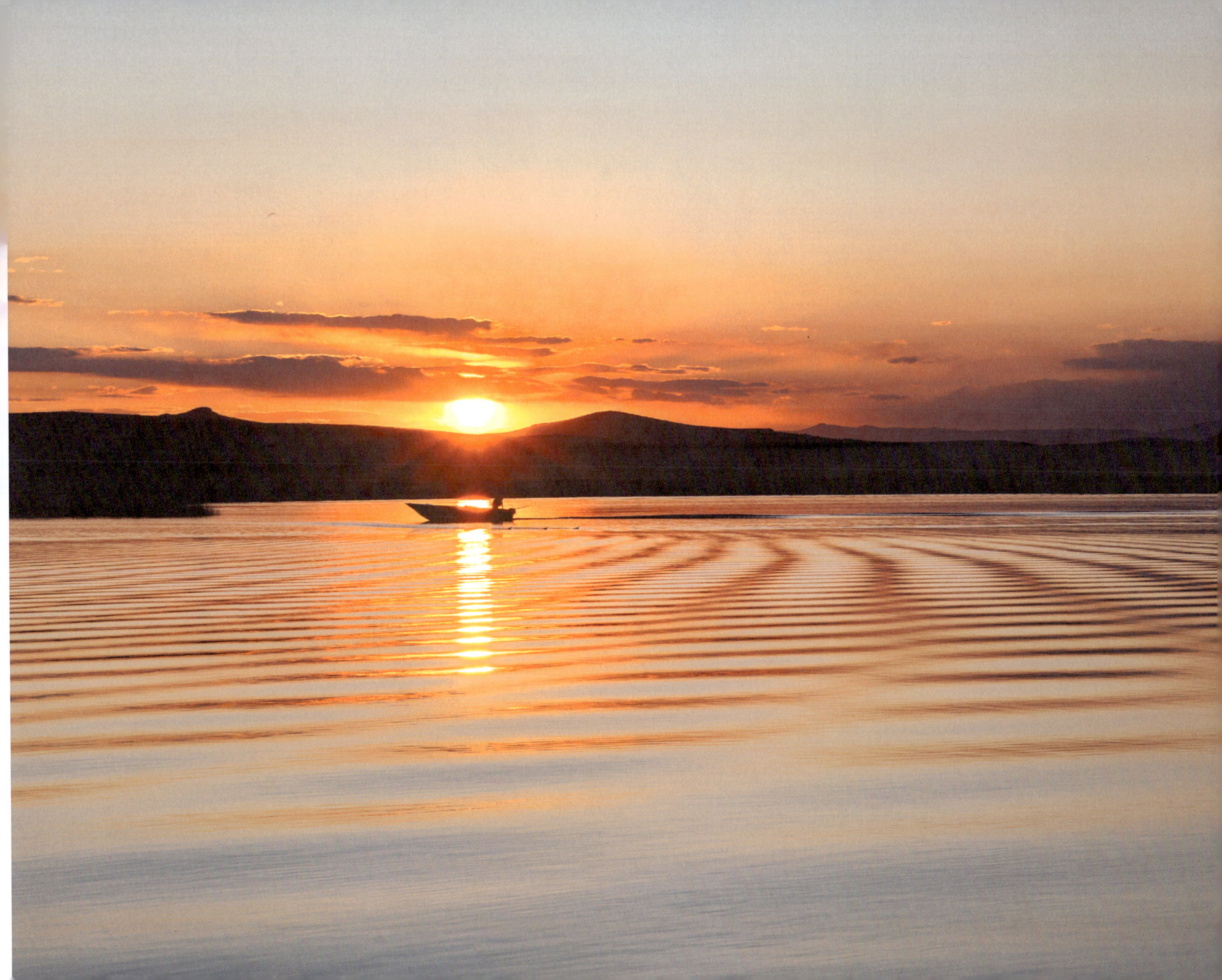

Relationships and Friends

It's sad that the pressures of a relationship usually end up destroying it.
You must be conscious of the other person's feelings all the time, which is good,
but you can become so obsessed with making that other person happy that you become miserable.

Niceties become obligations,
obligations lead to expectations,
failed expectations turn into hurt feelings and emotional scars that never heal,
the past becomes more vivid than the present
the words, *"you always"*, or *"you never"* start to make their way into every conversation.

Memories of that first kiss keep you bobbing in a sea of turmoil until one day not even that can keep you afloat
and you drown

That relationship dies and as you drag yourself ashore you feel the waves pulling you back into a sea of despair.
Once out you sit on the shore looking back at a peaceful ocean wondering how something so calm and beautiful could torment you so.
You tiptoe to the edge and the waves playfully lap at your feet inviting you back.
Foolishly you dive right in only to be tossed and tumbled by the waves and thrown back onto the sand.

Cold, wet and shivering you sit looking out wondering if you should try again or should you turn inland.

What to do...
What to do...

Cold and alone staring at the ocean,
you finally look up to see your friends standing around you.
With a towel and a smile they help you up and together you walk along the shore
between the woods and the sea,

together.
Friends.

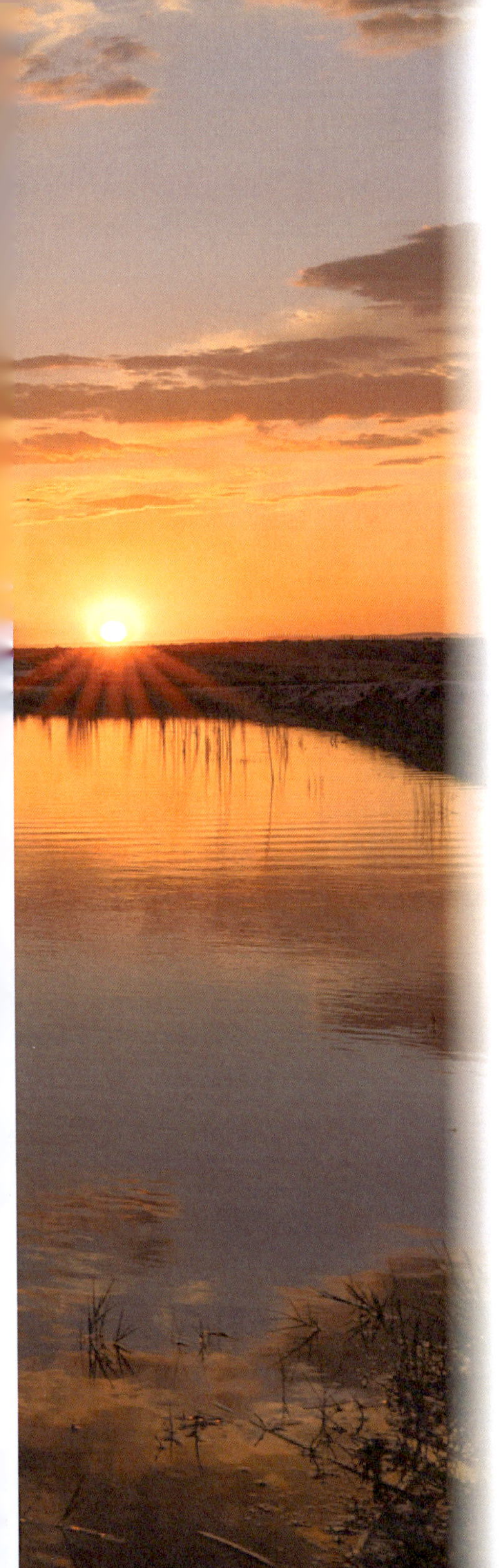

A hopeless romantic, that's how I've been described by others and myself admittedly. No matter how many times I get my heart broken or relationships fail I still keep jumping back in. I've also been called a slow learner, moron, and freaking idiot (in a loving way) by friends. Why do I keep doing the same thing over and over? Why do I jump into a situation I know is not good but insist that it will all work out in the end? Experience, logic, even a child's intuition, could tell me to turn and run the other direction but I stay and commit to a road that is clearly leading off a cliff with no exits. Maybe it's the hell I know vs. the fear of the unknown. Maybe I've grown comfortable in my discomfort zone. Maybe this one last time has finally taught me something.

When relationships are failing it is easy to feel like you're all alone. But you just have to stop and look around to see all your friends waiting to lend a hand. Take their hand, let them lift you back up. Remember, between the deep turbulent ocean and dark jungle

forest there is a beautiful sunny beach. Enjoy it with your friends.

Acknowledgement

I'd like to acknowledge all those who inspired the works you read here today: Ericka, Eileen, Christine, Elva, Rita, Kattia and Ileana.

To my dear friends and the remarkable models who appear on these pages, thank you for lending your essence to this work. Your presence brings these poems to life in ways beyond words.

@colcorama

@love_live_truc

@delkyra

@ileanachasephotography

Gerald Berliner for "I Heart Nature"

And to all those I've never met yet was moved by their presence.